2025
Air Fryer Cookbook
for Beginners UK

1900 Days of Super Quick, Delicious, and Kid-Friendly Recipe Book with Easy Instructions to Make Meal Prep Fast, Fun, and Tasty for Everyone

Elvinara Boranhanoglu

TABLE OF CONTENTS

INTRODUCTION

Introducing the Air Fryer Cookbook—the ultimate guide to creating mouthwatering, crispy, and healthier dishes with your air fryer. Imagine sinking your teeth into golden fries, juicy chicken, and even tempting desserts, all prepared with little to no oil. This cookbook is your go-to resource for making indulgent meals without the guilt.

Air frying is more than just a cooking method—it's a culinary revolution. In the Air Fryer Cookbook, we'll show you how to take your meals to the next level by creating perfectly crispy, flavorful dishes in less time and with fewer calories. From quick snacks to hearty dinners, this book has everything you need to transform your air fryer into a kitchen powerhouse.

What makes this cookbook special is its ability to guide you through the fundamentals of air frying while giving you the freedom to experiment and explore. Learn how to cook a variety of ingredients to perfection, with tips for achieving the ideal crispiness every time. Discover exciting seasoning and marinade combinations that will elevate your meals and make them more flavorful than ever before.

The Air Fryer Cookbook doesn't stop at just frying; we'll show you how versatile your air fryer can be. Roast, bake, and even grill your favorite dishes all in one convenient appliance. Plus, with step-by-step instructions, time-saving tips, and maintenance advice, you'll be an air frying expert in no time.

Are you ready to take your cooking to new heights? Let the Air Fryer Cookbook be your guide as you discover a world of crispy, delicious, and healthier meals. Whether you're cooking for yourself or entertaining guests, this book will help you create dishes that are sure to impress. Get ready to experience the joy of air frying—where every bite is a sensation!

Elevate Your Cooking with an Air Fryer

What if you could enjoy crispy, flavorful foods without the guilt? Enter the air fryer—a game-changing appliance that lets you indulge in your favorite fried foods while using up to 80% less oil. With its unique air circulation technology, the air fryer ensures your food is cooked to perfection—crispy on the outside, tender on the inside—all while maintaining a healthier cooking style. It's no wonder air fryers have become the must-have kitchen gadget for home cooks everywhere.

The Air Fryer Revolution: A New Era of Cooking

Air frying isn't just a passing trend—it's a revolutionary shift in the way we prepare meals. While the concept of cooking with hot air isn't new, it wasn't until the 2010s that air fryers became widely available. What started as a simple alternative to deep frying has grown into a multifunctional kitchen appliance capable of roasting, baking, and grilling. Modern air fryers now come with digital controls, presets for popular dishes, and even accessories to enhance their versatility.

Why Air Fryers Are Taking Over Kitchens Worldwide

The popularity of air fryers is undeniable,

and for good reason:

Healthier Fried Foods: Air fryers allow you to enjoy fried favorites—like crispy fries, chicken wings, and even donuts—without all the excess oil. This results in a significantly lower calorie count, making it easier to eat healthily without sacrificing flavor.

Versatility in the Kitchen: Air fryers do more than just fry! They can roast, bake, grill, and even reheat leftovers. Whether you're cooking veggies, baking a cake, or preparing a batch of crispy chicken, the air fryer can handle it all with ease.

Speed and Convenience: Thanks to its rapid air circulation, the air fryer cooks meals faster than traditional ovens, making it perfect for busy days. Preheating takes seconds, and many models are equipped with simple controls that make meal prep effortless.

Even Cooking Every Time: Air fryers provide consistent, even cooking thanks to their efficient hot air circulation system. You'll get perfectly crispy results with every dish, whether it's a quick snack or a full meal.

Effortless Cleanup: With their non-stick baskets and removable trays, air fryers are a breeze to clean. Many parts are dishwasher-safe, saving you time and effort after cooking.

Minimal Odor and Smoke: Unlike traditional frying methods, air fryers produce little to no smoke, meaning your kitchen stays clean and fresh during and after cooking. Say goodbye to greasy smells lingering in the air!

Compact and Stylish: Air fryers are designed to take up minimal counter space while adding a sleek, modern touch to your kitchen. Their compact size makes them ideal for small spaces and easy to store when not in use.

Air Fryer Essentials: Tips for Getting Started

Preheat for Perfection: Just like an oven, preheating your air fryer is crucial. It helps the appliance reach the right temperature for even cooking, ensuring crispy and delicious results.

Give Your Food Room: Avoid overcrowding the basket. When food is spaced out, the hot air can circulate more effectively, ensuring an even cook and perfect crispness.

Shake or Turn Halfway: For even browning, shake or flip the food halfway through the cooking time. This helps to expose all sides to the hot air, creating a more consistent and crispy texture.

Use Oil Sparingly: Air fryers require less oil, but a light spray or drizzle can enhance the flavor and texture. Apply just enough to give your food a crispy exterior without excess grease.

Customize Your Settings: Not every air fryer cooks the same, so take time to experiment with temperature and time settings based on the food you're preparing. Adjusting these to your preferences will ensure the best results.

Clean Regularly: Keeping your air fryer clean is key to maintaining its efficiency. After each use, wipe down the basket and tray, and periodically deep clean according to the manufacturer's instructions to keep it running smoothly.

By following these straightforward tips, you'll quickly master your air fryer and enjoy delicious, healthy meals with minimal effort!

Egg Tarts

Preparation time: 10 minutes | Cook time: 17 to 20 minutes | Makes 2 tarts

- ⅓ sheet frozen puff pastry, thawed
- Cooking oil spray
- 120 g grated Cheddar cheese
- 2 eggs
- ¼ teaspoon salt, divided
- 1 teaspoon minced fresh parsley (optional)

Instructions

1. Insert the crisper plate into the basket and the basket into the unit. Preheat the unit by selecting BAKE, setting the temperature to 200°C, and setting the time to 3 minutes. Select START/STOP to begin. 2. Lay the puff pastry sheet on a piece of parchment paper and cut it in half. 3. Once the unit is preheated, spray the crisper plate with cooking oil. Transfer the 2 squares of pastry to the basket, keeping them on the parchment paper. 4. Select BAKE, set the temperature to 200°C, and set the time to 20 minutes. Select START/STOP to begin. 5. After 10 minutes, use a metal spoon to press down the center of each pastry square to make a well. Divide the cheese equally between the baked pastries. Carefully crack an egg on top of the cheese, and sprinkle each with the salt. Resume cooking for 7 to 10 minutes. 6. When the cooking is complete, the eggs will be cooked through. Sprinkle each with parsley (if using) and serve.

Garlicky Olive Stromboli

Preparation time: 25 minutes | Cook time: 25 minutes | Serves 8

- 4 large cloves garlic, unpeeled
- 3 tablespoons grated Parmesan cheese
- 120 g packed fresh basil leaves
- 120 g marinated, pitted green and black olives
- ¼ teaspoon crushed red pepper
- 230 g pizza dough, at room temperature
- 110 g sliced provolone cheese (about 8 slices)
- Cooking spray

Instructions

1. Preheat the air fryer to 190°C 2.Spritz the air fryer basket with cooking spray 3.Put the unpeeled garlic in the air fryer basket 4.Air fry for 10 minutes or until the garlic is softened completely 5.Remove them from the air fryer and allow to cool until you can handle 6.Peel the garlic and place into a food processor with 2 tablespoons of Parmesan, basil, olives, and crushed red pepper 7.Pulse to mix well 8.Set aside 9.Arrange the pizza dough on a clean work surface, then roll it out with a rolling pin into a rectangle 10.Cut the rectangle in half 1Instructions

1.Sprinkle half of the garlic mixture over each rectangle half and leave ½-inch edges uncover 12.Top them with the provolone cheese 13.Brush one long side of each rectangle half with water, then roll them up 14.Spritz the air fryer basket with cooking spray 15.Transfer the rolls in the preheated air fryer 16.Spritz with cooking spray and scatter with remaining Parmesan 17.Air fry the rolls for 15 minutes or until golden brown 18.Flip the rolls halfway through 19.Remove the rolls from the air fryer and allow to cool for a few minutes before serving.

Maple Muesli

Preparation time: 5 minutes | Cook

time: 40 minutes | Makes 475 ml

- 235 g porridge oats
- 3 tablespoons pure maple syrup
- 1 tablespoon sugar
- 1 tablespoon neutral-flavoured oil, such as refined coconut or sunflower
- ¼ teaspoon sea salt
- ¼ teaspoon ground cinnamon
- ¼ teaspoon vanilla extract

Instructions

1. Insert the crisper plate into the basket and the basket into the unit. Preheat the unit by selecting BAKE, setting the temperature to 120ºC, and setting the time to 3 minutes. Select START/STOP to begin. 2. In a medium bowl, stir together the oats, maple syrup, sugar, oil, salt, cinnamon, and vanilla until thoroughly combined. Transfer the muesli to a 6-by-2-inch round baking pan. 3. Once the unit is preheated, place the pan into the basket. 4. Select BAKE, set the temperature to 120ºC and set the time to 40 minutes. Select START/STOP to begin. 5. After 10 minutes, stir the muesli well. Resume cooking, stirring the muesli every 10 minutes, for a total of 40 minutes, or until the muesli is lightly browned and mostly dry. 6. When the cooking is complete, place the muesli on a plate to cool. It will become crisp as it cools. Store the completely cooled muesli in an airtight container in a cool, dry place for 1 to 2 weeks.

Hole in One

Preparation time: 5 minutes | Cook time: 6 to 7 minutes | Serves 1

- 1 slice bread
- 1 teaspoon soft butter
- 1 egg
- Salt and pepper, to taste
- 1 tablespoon grated Cheddar cheese
- 2 teaspoons diced gammon

Instructions

1. Place a baking dish inside air fryer basket and preheat the air fryer to 170ºC. 2. Using a 2½-inch-diameter biscuit cutter, cut a hole in center of bread slice. 3. Spread softened butter on both sides of bread. 4. Lay bread slice in baking dish and crack egg into the hole. Sprinkle egg with salt and pepper to taste. 5. Cook for 5 minutes. 6. Turn toast over and top it with grated cheese and diced gammon. 7. Cook for 1 to 2 more minutes or until yolk is done to your liking.

Bacon Eggs on the Go

Preparation time: 5 minutes | Cook time: 15 minutes | Serves 1

- 2 eggs
- 110 g bacon, cooked
- Salt and ground black pepper, to taste

Instructions

1. Preheat the air fryer to 200ºC. Put liners in a regular cupcake tin. 2. Crack an egg into each of the cups and add the bacon. Season with some pepper and salt. 3. Bake in the preheated air fryer for 15 minutes, or until the eggs are set. Serve warm.

Tomato and Mozzarella Bruschetta

Preparation time: 5 minutes | Cook time: 4 minutes | Serves 1

- 6 small loaf slices
- 120 g tomatoes, finely chopped
- 85 g Cheddar cheese, grated
- 1 tablespoon fresh basil, chopped
- 1 tablespoon rapeseed oil

Instructions

1. Preheat the air fryer to 180ºC. 2. Put the loaf slices inside the air fryer and air fry for about 3 minutes. 3. Add the tomato, Mozzarella, basil, and rapeseed oil on top. 4. Air fry for an additional minute before serving.

Hearty Cheddar Biscuits

Preparation time: 10 minutes | Cook time: 22 minutes | Makes 8 biscuits

- 250 g self-raising flour
- 2 tablespoons sugar
- 120 g butter, frozen for 15 minutes
- 120 g grated Cheddar cheese, plus more to melt on top
- 315 ml buttermilk
- 235 g plain flour, for shaping
- 1 tablespoon butter, melted

Instructions

1. Line a buttered 7-inch metal cake pan with parchment paper or a silicone liner. 2. Combine the flour and sugar in a large mixing bowl. Grate the butter into the flour. Add the grated cheese and stir to coat the cheese and butter with flour. Then add the buttermilk and stir just until you tin no longer see streaks of flour. The dough should be quite wet. 3. Spread the plain (not self-raising) flour out on a small baking sheet. With a spoon, scoop 8 evenly sized balls of dough into the flour, making sure they don't touch each other. With floured hands, coat each dough ball with flour and toss them gently from hand to hand to shake off any excess flour. Put each floured dough ball into the prepared pan, right up next to the other. This will help the biscuits rise, rather than spreading out. 4. Preheat the air fryer to 190°C. 5. Transfer the cake pan to the basket of the air fryer. Let the ends of the aluminium foil sling hang across the cake pan before returning the basket to the air fryer. 6. Air fry for 20 minutes. Check the biscuits twice to make sure they are not getting too brown on top. If they are, re-arrange the aluminium foil strips to cover any brown parts. After 20 minutes, check the biscuits by inserting a toothpick into the center of the biscuits. It should come out clean. If it needs a little more time, continue to air fry for two extra minutes. Brush the tops of the biscuits with some melted butter and sprinkle a little more grated cheese on top if desired. Pop the basket back into the air fryer for another 2 minutes. 7. Remove the cake pan from the air fryer. Let the biscuits cool for just a minute or two and then turn them out onto a plate and pull apart. Serve immediately.

Western Frittata

Preparation time: 10 minutes | Cook time: 19 minutes | Serves 1 to 2

- ½ red or green pepper, cut into ½-inch chunks
- 1 teaspoon rapeseed oil
- 3 eggs, beaten
- 60 g grated Cheddar cheese
- 60 g diced cooked gammon
- Salt and freshly ground black pepper, to taste
- 1 teaspoon butter
- 1 teaspoon chopped fresh parsley

Instructions

1. Preheat the air fryer to 200°C. 2. Toss the peppers with the rapeseed oil and air fry for 6 minutes, shaking the basket once or twice during the cooking process to redistribute the ingredients. 3. While the vegetables are cooking, beat the eggs well in a bowl, stir in the Cheddar cheese and gammon, and season with salt and freshly ground black pepper. Add the air-fried peppers to this bowl when they have finished cooking. 4. Place a cake pan into the air fryer basket with the butter using an aluminum sling to lower the pan into the basket. Air fry for 1 minute at 190°C to melt the butter. Remove the cake pan and rotate the pan to distribute the butter and grease the pan. Pour the egg mixture into the cake pan and return the pan to the air fryer, using the aluminum sling. 5. Air fry at 190°C for 12 minutes, or until the frittata has puffed up and is lightly browned. Let the frittata sit in the air fryer for 5 minutes to cool to an edible temperature and set up. Remove the cake pan from the air fryer, sprinkle with

parsley and serve immediately.

All-in-One Toast

Preparation time: 10 minutes | Cook time: 10 minutes | Serves 1

- ✧ 1 strip bacon, diced
- ✧ 1 slice 1-inch thick bread
- ✧ 1 egg
- ✧ Salt and freshly ground black pepper, to taste
- ✧ 60 g grated Monterey Jack or Chedday cheese

Instructions

1. Preheat the air fryer to 200ºC. 2. Air fry the bacon for 3 minutes, shaking the basket once or twice while it cooks. Remove the bacon to a paper towel lined plate and set aside. 3. Use a sharp paring knife to score a large circle in the middle of the slice of bread, cutting halfway through, but not all the way through to the cutting board. Press down on the circle in the center of the bread slice to create an indentation. 4. Transfer the slice of bread, hole side up, to the air fryer basket. Crack the egg into the center of the bread, and season with salt and pepper. 5. Adjust the air fryer temperature to 190ºC and air fry for 5 minutes. Sprinkle the grated cheese around the edges of the bread, leaving the center of the yolk uncovered, and top with the cooked bacon. Press the cheese and bacon into the bread lightly to help anchor it to the bread and prevent it from blowing around in the air fryer. 6. Air fry for one or two more minutes, just to melt the cheese and finish cooking the egg. Serve immediately.

Cinnamon Rolls

Preparation time: 10 minutes | Cook time: 20 minutes | Makes 12 rolls

- ✧ 600 g grated Cheddar cheese
- ✧ 60 g soft cheese, softened
- ✧ 120 g blanched finely ground almond flour
- ✧ ½ teaspoon vanilla extract
- ✧ 96 ml icing sugar-style sweetener
- ✧ 1 tablespoon ground cinnamon

Instructions

1. In a large microwave-safe bowl, combine Cheddar cheese, soft cheese, and flour. Microwave the mixture on high 90 seconds until cheese is melted. 2. Add vanilla extract and sweetener, and mix 2 minutes until a dough forms. 3. Once the dough is cool enough to work with your hands, about 2 minutes, spread it out into a 12 × 4-inch rectangle on ungreased parchment paper. Evenly sprinkle dough with cinnamon. 4. Starting at the long side of the dough, roll lengthwise to form a log. Slice the log into twelve even pieces. 5. Divide rolls between two ungreased round nonstick baking dishes. Place one dish into air fryer basket. Adjust the temperature to 190ºC and bake for 10 minutes. 6. Cinnamon rolls will be done when golden around the edges and mostly firm. Repeat with second dish. Allow rolls to cool in dishes 10 minutes before serving.

Lemon-Blueberry Muffins

Preparation time: 5 minutes | Cook time: 20 to 25 minutes | Makes 6 muffins

- ✧ 150 g almond flour
- ✧ 3 tablespoons granulated sweetener
- ✧ 1 teaspoon baking powder
- ✧ 2 large eggs
- ✧ 3 tablespoons melted butter
- ✧ 1 tablespoon almond milk
- ✧ 1 tablespoon fresh lemon juice
- ✧ 120 g fresh blueberries

Instructions

1. Preheat the air fryer to 180ºC. Lightly coat 6 silicone muffin cups with vegetable oil. Set aside. 2. In a large mixing bowl, combine the almond flour, sweetener, and baking soda. Set aside. 3. In a separate small bowl, whisk

together the eggs, butter, milk, and lemon juice. Add the egg mixture to the flour mixture and stir until just combined. Fold in the blueberries and let the batter sit for 5 minutes. 4. Spoon the muffin batter into the muffin cups, about two-thirds full. Air fry for 20 to 25 minutes, or until a toothpick inserted into the center of a muffin comes out clean. 5. Remove the basket from the air fryer and let the muffins cool for about 5 minutes before transferring them to a wire rack to cool completely.

Mozzarella Bacon Calzones

Preparation time: 15 minutes | Cook time: 12 minutes | Serves 4

- ✧ 2 large eggs
- ✧ 120 g blanched finely ground almond flour
- ✧ 475 g grated Cheddar cheese
- ✧ 60 g soft cheese, softened and broken into small pieces
- ✧ 4 slices cooked bacon, crumbled

Instructions

1. Beat eggs in a small bowl. Pour into a medium nonstick frying pan over medium heat and scramble. Set aside. 2. In a large microwave-safe bowl, mix flour and Mozzarella. Add soft cheese to the bowl. 3. Place bowl in microwave and cook 45 seconds on high to melt cheese, then stir with a fork until a soft dough ball forms. 4. Cut a piece of parchment to fit air fryer basket. Separate dough into two sections and press each out into an 8-inch round. 5. On half of each dough round, place half of the scrambled eggs and crumbled bacon. Fold the other side of the dough over and press to seal the edges. 6. Place calzones on ungreased parchment and into air fryer basket. Adjust the temperature to 180ºC and set the timer for 12 minutes, turning calzones halfway through cooking. Crust will be golden and firm when done. 7. Let calzones cool on a cooking rack 5 minutes before serving.

Vanilla Muesli

Preparation time: 5 minutes | Cook time: 40 minutes | Serves 4

- ✧ 235 g porridge oats
- ✧ 3 tablespoons maple syrup
- ✧ 1 tablespoon sunflower oil
- ✧ 1 tablespoon coconut sugar
- ✧ ¼ teaspoon vanilla
- ✧ ¼ teaspoon cinnamon
- ✧ ¼ teaspoon sea salt

Instructions

1. Preheat the air fryer to 120ºC. 2. Mix together the oats, maple syrup, sunflower oil, coconut sugar, vanilla, cinnamon, and sea salt in a medium bowl and stir to combine. Transfer the mixture to a baking pan. 3. Place the pan in the air fryer basket and bake for 40 minutes, or until the muesli is mostly dry and lightly browned. Stir the muesli four times during cooking. 4. Let the muesli stand for 5 to 10 minutes before serving.

Banger and Egg Breakfast Burrito

Preparation time: 5 minutes | Cook time: 30 minutes | Serves 6

- ✧ 6 eggs
- ✧ Salt and pepper, to taste
- ✧ Cooking oil
- ✧ 120 g chopped red pepper
- ✧ 120 g chopped green pepper
- ✧ 230 g chicken banger meat (removed from casings)
- ✧ 120 ml tomato salsa
- ✧ 6 medium (8-inch) wheat maize wraps
- ✧ 120 g grated Cheddar cheese

Instructions

1. In a medium bowl, whisk the eggs. Add salt and pepper to taste. 2. Place a frying pan on medium-high heat. Spray with cooking oil. Add the eggs. Scramble for 2 to 3 minutes, until the eggs are fluffy. Remove the eggs

from the frying pan and set aside. 3. If needed, spray the frying pan with more oil. Add the chopped red and green peppers. Cook for 2 to 3 minutes, until the peppers are soft. 4. Add the banger meat to the frying pan. Break the banger into smaller pieces using a spatula or spoon. Cook for 3 to 4 minutes, until the banger is brown. 5. Add the tomato salsa and scrambled eggs. Stir to combine. Remove the frying pan from heat. 6. Spoon the mixture evenly onto the maize wraps. 7. To form the burritos, fold the sides of each maize wrap in toward the middle and then roll up from the bottom. You tin secure each burrito with a toothpick. Or you tin moisten the outside edge of the maize wrap with a small amount of water. I prefer to use a cooking brush, but you tin also dab with your fingers. 8. Spray the burritos with cooking oil and place them in the air fryer. Do not stack. Cook the burritos in batches if they do not all fit in the basket. Air fry at 200°C for 8 minutes. 9. Open the air fryer and flip the burritos. Cook for an additional 2 minutes or until crisp. 10. If necessary, repeat steps 8 and 9 for the remaining burritos. 1Instructions

1. Sprinkle the Cheddar cheese over the burritos. Cool before serving.

Cheesy Scrambled Eggs

Preparation time: 2 minutes | Cook time: 9 minutes | Serves 2

- ✧ 1 teaspoon unsalted butter
- ✧ 2 large eggs
- ✧ 2 tablespoons milk
- ✧ 2 tablespoons grated Cheddar cheese
- ✧ Salt and freshly ground black pepper, to taste

Instructions

1. Preheat the air fryer to 150°C. Place the butter in a baking pan and cook for 1 to 2 minutes, until melted. 2. In a small bowl, whisk together the eggs, milk, and cheese.

Season with salt and black pepper. Transfer the mixture to the pan. 3. Cook for 3 minutes. Stir the eggs and push them toward themaize center of the pan. 4. Cook for another 2 minutes, then stir again. Cook for another 2 minutes, until the eggs are just cooked. Serve warm.

Bacon and Spinach Egg Muffins

Preparation time: 7 minutes | Cook time: 12 to 14 minutes | Serves 6

- ✧ 6 large eggs
- ✧ 60 ml double (whipping) cream
- ✧ ½ teaspoon sea salt
- ✧ ¼ teaspoon freshly ground black pepper
- ✧ ¼ teaspoon cayenne pepper (optional)
- ✧ 180 g frozen chopped spinach, thawed and drained
- ✧ 4 strips cooked bacon, crumbled
- ✧ 60 g grated Cheddar cheese

Instructions

1. In a large bowl (with a spout if you have one), whisk together the eggs, double cream, salt, black pepper, and cayenne pepper (if using). 2. Divide the spinach and bacon among 6 silicone muffin cups. Place the muffin cups in your air fryer basket. 3. Divide the egg mixture among the muffin cups. Top with the cheese. 4. Set the air fryer to 150°C. Bake for 12 to 14 minutes, until the eggs are set and cooked through.

Buffalo Chicken Breakfast Muffins

Preparation time: 7 minutes | Cook time: 13 to 16 minutes | Serves 10

- ✧ 170 g grated cooked chicken
- ✧ 85 g blue cheese, crumbled
- ✧ 2 tablespoons unsalted butter, melted
- ✧ 80 ml Buffalo hot sauce, such as Frank's RedHot
- ✧ 1 teaspoon minced garlic
- ✧ 6 large eggs

- ✧ Sea salt and freshly ground black pepper, to taste
- ✧ Avocado oil spray

Instructions

1. In a large bowl, stir together the chicken, blue cheese, melted butter, hot sauce, and garlic. 2. In a medium bowl or large liquid measuring cup, beat the eggs. Season with salt and pepper. 3. Spray 10 silicone muffin cups with oil. Divide the chicken mixture among the cups, and pour the egg mixture over top. 4. Place the cups in the air fryer and set to 150ºC. Bake for 13 to 16 minutes, until the muffins are set and cooked through. (Depending on the size of your air fryer, you may need to cook the muffins in batches.)

Green Eggs and Gammon

Preparation time: 5 minutes | Cook time: 10 minutes | Serves 2

- ✧ 1 large Hass avocado, halved and pitted
- ✧ 2 thin slices gammon
- ✧ 2 large eggs
- ✧ 2 tablespoons chopped spring onions, plus more for garnish
- ✧ ½ teaspoon fine sea salt
- ✧ ¼ teaspoon ground black pepper
- ✧ 60 g grated Cheddar cheese (omit for dairy-free)

Instructions

1. Preheat the air fryer to 200ºC. 2. Place a slice of gammon into the cavity of each avocado half. Crack an egg on top of the gammon, then sprinkle on the spring onions, salt, and pepper. 3. Place the avocado halves in the air fryer cut side up and air fry for 10 minutes, or until the egg is cooked to your desired doneness. Top with the cheese (if using) and air fry for 30 seconds more, or until the cheese is melted. Garnish with chopped spring onions. 4. Best served fresh. Store extras in an airtight container in the fridge for up to 4 days. Reheat in a preheated 180ºC air fryer for a few minutes, until

warmed through.

Eggnog Bread

Preparation time: 10 minutes | Cook time: 18 minutes | Serves 6 to 8

- ✧ 120 g flour, plus more for dusting
- ✧ 35 g sugar
- ✧ 1 teaspoon baking powder
- ✧ ¼ teaspoon salt
- ✧ ¼ teaspoon nutmeg
- ✧ 120 ml eggnog
- ✧ 1 egg yolk
- ✧ 1 tablespoon plus 1 teaspoon butter, melted
- ✧ 60 g pecans
- ✧ 60 g chopped candied fruit (cherries, pineapple, or mixed fruits)
- ✧ Cooking spray

Instructions

1. Preheat the air fryer to 180ºC 2.In a medium bowl, stir together the flour, sugar, baking powder, salt, and nutmeg 3.Add eggnog, egg yolk, and butter 4.Mix well but do not beat 5.Stir in nuts and fruit 6.Spray a baking dish with cooking spray and dust with flour 7.Spread batter into prepared pan and bake for 18 minutes or until top is dark golden brown and bread starts to pull away from sides of pan 8.Serve immediately.

Southwestern Gammon Egg Cups

Preparation time: 5 minutes | Cook time: 12 minutes | Serves 2

- ✧ 4 (30 g) slices wafer-thin gammon
- ✧ 4 large eggs
- ✧ 2 tablespoons full-fat sour cream
- ✧ 60 g diced green pepper
- ✧ 2 tablespoons diced red pepper
- ✧ 2 tablespoons diced brown onion
- ✧ 120 g grated medium Cheddar cheese

Instructions

1. Place one slice of gammon on the bottom of four baking cups. 2. In a large bowl, whisk eggs with sour cream. Stir in green pepper,

red pepper, and onion. 3. Pour the egg mixture into gammon-lined baking cups. Top with Cheddar. Place cups into the air fryer basket. 4. Adjust the temperature to 160°C and bake for 12 minutes or until the tops are browned. 5. Serve warm.

Hearty Blueberry Porridge

Preparation time: 10 minutes | Cook time: 25 minutes | Serves 6

✧ 350 g porridge oats
✧ 1¼ teaspoons ground cinnamon, divided
✧ ½ teaspoon baking powder
✧ Pinch salt
✧ 235 ml unsweetened vanilla almond milk
✧ 60 ml honey
✧ 1 teaspoon vanilla extract
✧ 1 egg, beaten
✧ 475 g blueberries
✧ vegetable oil (such as rapeseed oil)
✧ 1½ teaspoons sugar, divided
✧ 6 tablespoons low-fat whipped topping (optional)

Instructions

1. In a large bowl, mix together the oats, 1 teaspoon of cinnamon, baking powder, and salt. 2. In a medium bowl, whisk together the almond milk, honey, vanilla and egg. 3. Pour the liquid ingredients into the oats mixture and stir to combine. Fold in the blueberries. 4. Lightly spray a baking pan with oil. 5. Add half the blueberry mixture to the pan. 6. Sprinkle ⅛ teaspoon of cinnamon and ½ teaspoon sugar over the top. 7. Cover the pan with aluminium foil and place gently in the air fryer basket. 8. Air fry at 180°C for 20 minutes. Remove the foil and air fry for an additional 5 minutes. Transfer the mixture to a shallow bowl. 9. Repeat with the remaining blueberry mixture, ½ teaspoon of sugar, and ⅛ teaspoon of cinnamon. 10. To serve, spoon into bowls and top with whipped topping.

Bacon, Egg, and Cheese Roll Ups

Preparation time: 15 minutes | Cook time: 15 minutes | Serves 4

✧ 2 tablespoons unsalted butter
✧ 60 g chopped onion
✧ ½ medium green pepper, seeded and chopped
✧ 6 large eggs
✧ 12 slices bacon
✧ 235 g grated mature Cheddar cheese
✧ 120 ml mild tomato salsa, for dipping

Instructions

1. In a medium frying pan over medium heat, melt butter. Add onion and pepper to the frying pan and sauté until fragrant and onions are translucent, about 3 minutes. 2. Whisk eggs in a small bowl and pour into frying pan. Scramble eggs with onions and peppers until fluffy and fully cooked, about 5 minutes. Remove from heat and set aside. 3. On work surface, place three slices of bacon side by side, overlapping about ¼ inch. Place 60 ml scrambled eggs in a heap on the side closest to you and sprinkle 60 ml cheese on top of the eggs. 4. Tightly roll the bacon around the eggs and secure the seam with a toothpick if necessary. Place each roll into the air fryer basket. 5. Adjust the temperature to 180°C and air fry for 15 minutes. Rotate the rolls halfway through the cooking time. 6. Bacon will be brown and crispy when completely cooked. Serve immediately with tomato salsa for dipping.

Personal Cauliflower Pizzas

Preparation time: 10 minutes | Cook time: 25 minutes | Serves 2

✧ 1 (340 g) bag frozen riced cauliflower
✧ 75 g shredded Mozzarella cheese
✧ 15 g almond flour
✧ 20 g Parmesan cheese
✧ 1 large egg
✧ ½ teaspoon salt
✧ 1 teaspoon garlic powder
✧ 1 teaspoon dried oregano
✧ 4 tablespoons no-sugar-added marinara sauce, divided
✧ 110 g fresh Mozzarella, chopped, divided
✧ 140 g cooked chicken breast, chopped, divided
✧ 100 g chopped cherry tomatoes, divided
✧ 5 g fresh baby rocket, divided

Instructions

1. Preheat the air fryer to 200°C. Cut 4 sheets of parchment paper to fit the basket of the air fryer. Brush with olive oil and set aside. 2. In a large glass bowl, microwave the cauliflower according to package directions. Place the cauliflower on a clean towel, draw up the sides, and squeeze tightly over a sink to remove the excess moisture. Return the cauliflower to the bowl and add the shredded Mozzarella along with the almond flour, Parmesan, egg, salt, garlic powder, and oregano. Stir until thoroughly combined. 3. Divide the dough into two equal portions. Place one piece of dough on the prepared parchment paper and pat gently into a thin, flat disk 7 to 8 inches in diameter. Air fry for 15 minutes until the crust begins to brown. Let cool for 5 minutes. 4. Transfer the parchment paper with the crust on top to a baking sheet. Place a second sheet of parchment paper over the crust. While holding the edges of both sheets together, carefully lift the crust off the baking sheet, flip it, and place it back in the air fryer basket. The new sheet of parchment paper is now on the bottom. Remove the top piece of paper and air fry the crust for another 15 minutes until the top begins to brown. Remove the basket from the air fryer. 5. Spread 2 tablespoons of the marinara sauce on top of the crust, followed by half the fresh Mozzarella, chicken, cherry tomatoes, and rocket. Air fry for 5 to 10 minutes longer, until the cheese is melted and beginning to brown. Remove the pizza from the oven and let it sit for 10 minutes before serving. Repeat with the remaining ingredients to make a second pizza.

Pork Burgers with Red Cabbage Salad

Preparation time: 20 minutes | Cook time: 7 to 9 minutes | Serves 4

✧ 120 ml Greek yoghurt
✧ 2 tablespoons low-salt mustard, divided
✧ 1 tablespoon lemon juice
✧ 60 g sliced red cabbage
✧ 60 g grated carrots
✧ 450 g lean finely chopped pork
✧ ½ teaspoon paprika
✧ 235 g mixed salad leaves
✧ 2 small tomatoes, sliced
✧ 8 small low-salt wholemeal sandwich buns, cut in half

Instructions

1. In a small bowl, combine the yoghurt, 1 tablespoon mustard, lemon juice, cabbage, and carrots; mix and refrigerate. 2.In a medium bowl, combine the pork, remaining 1

tablespoon mustard, and paprika. Form into 8 small patties. Put the sliders into the air fryer basket. 3.Air fry at 200°C for 7 to 9 minutes, or until the sliders register 74°C as tested with a meat thermometer. 4.Assemble the burgers by placing some of the lettuce greens on a bun bottom. 5.Top with a tomato slice, the burgers, and the cabbage mixture. 6.Add the bun top and serve immediately.

Avocado and Egg Burrito

Preparation time: 10 minutes | Cook time: 3 to 5 minutes | Serves 4

- 2 hard-boiled egg whites, chopped
- 1 hard-boiled egg, chopped
- 1 avocado, peeled, pitted, and chopped
- 1 red pepper, chopped
- 3 tablespoons low-salt salsa, plus additional for serving (optional)
- 1 (34 g) slice low-salt, low-fat processed cheese, torn into pieces
- 4 low-salt wholemeal flour wraps

Instructions

1. In a medium bowl, thoroughly mix the egg whites, egg, avocado, red pepper, salsa, and cheese. 2.Place the maize wraps on a work surface and evenly divide the filling among them. 3.Fold in the edges and roll up. Secure the burritos with toothpicks if necessary. 4.Put the burritos in the air fryer basket. 5.Air fry at 200°C for 3 to 5 minutes, or until the burritos are light golden brown and crisp. 6.Serve with more salsa (if using).

Cheesy Roasted Sweet Potatoes

Preparation time: 7 minutes | Cook time: 18 to 23 minutes | Serves 4

- 2 large sweet potatoes, peeled and sliced
- 1 teaspoon olive oil
- 1 tablespoon white balsamic vinegar
- 1 teaspoon dried thyme
- 60 g Parmesan cheese

Instructions

1. In a large bowl, drizzle the sweet potato slices with the olive oil and toss. 2.Sprinkle with the balsamic vinegar and thyme and toss again. 3.Sprinkle the potatoes with the Parmesan cheese and toss to coat. 4.Roast the slices, in batches, in the air fryer basket at 200°C for 18 to 23 minutes, tossing the sweet potato slices in the basket once during cooking, until tender. 5.Repeat with the remaining sweet potato slices. 6.Serve immediately.

Bacon-Wrapped Hot Dogs

Preparation time: 5 minutes | Cook time: 10 minutes | Serves 4

- Oil, for spraying
- 4 bacon rashers
- 4 hot dog bangers
- 4 hot dog rolls
- Toppings of choice

Instructions

1. Line the air fryer basket with parchment and spray lightly with oil. 2.Wrap a strip of bacon tightly around each hot dog, taking care to cover the tips so they don't get too crispy. 3.Secure with a toothpick at each end to keep the bacon from shrinking. 4.Place the hot dogs in the prepared basket. 5.Air fry at 190°C for 8 to 9 minutes, depending on how crispy you like the bacon. For extra-crispy, cook the hot dogs at 200°C for 6 to 8 minutes. 6.Place the hot dogs in the buns, return them to the air fryer, and cook for another 1 to 2 minutes, or until the buns are warm. 7.Add your desired toppings and serve.

Apple Pie Egg Rolls

Preparation time: 10 minutes | Cook time: 8 minutes | Makes 6 rolls

- Oil, for spraying
- 1 (600 g) tin apple pie filling
- 1 tablespoon plain flour
- ½ teaspoon lemon juice
- ¼ teaspoon ground nutmeg

✧ ¼ teaspoon ground cinnamon

✧ 6 egg roll wrappers

Instructions

1. Preheat the air fryer to 200°C. 2.Line the air fryer basket with parchment and spray lightly with oil. 3.In a medium bowl, mix together the pie filling, flour, lemon juice, nutmeg, and cinnamon. 4.Lay out the egg roll wrappers on a work surface and spoon a dollop of pie filling in the centre of each. 5.Fill a small bowl with water. Dip your finger in the water and, working one at a time, moisten the edges of the wrappers. 6.Fold the wrapper like an packet: First fold one corner into the centre. 7.Fold each side corner in, and then fold over the remaining corner, making sure each corner overlaps a bit and the moistened edges stay closed. 8.Use additional water and your fingers to seal any open edges. 9.Place the rolls in the prepared basket and spray liberally with oil. 10.You may need to work in batches, depending on the size of your air fryer. 1Instructions

1.Cook for 4 minutes, flip, spray with oil, and cook for another 4 minutes, or until crispy and golden brown. 12.Serve immediately.

Pork Stuffing Meatballs

Preparation time: 10 minutes | Cook time: 12 minutes | Makes 35 meatballs

✧ Oil, for spraying

✧ 680 g finely chopped pork

✧ 120 g breadcrumbs

✧ 120 ml milk

✧ 60 g finely chopped onion

✧ 1 large egg

✧ 1 tablespoon dried rosemary

✧ 1 tablespoon dried thyme

✧ 1 teaspoon salt

✧ 1 teaspoon ground black pepper

✧ 1 teaspoon finely chopped fresh parsley

Instructions

1. Line the air fryer basket with parchment and spray lightly with oil. 2.In a large bowl, mix together the finely chopped pork, breadcrumbs, milk, onion, egg, rosemary, thyme, salt, black pepper, and parsley. 3.Roll about 2 tablespoons of the mixture into a ball. 4.Repeat with the rest of the mixture. You should have 30 to 35 meatballs. 5.Place the meatballs in the prepared basket in a single layer, leaving space between each one. You may need to work in batches, depending on the size of your air fryer. 6.Air fry at 200°C for 10 to 12 minutes, flipping after 5 minutes, or until golden brown and the internal temperature reaches 72°C.

Steak Tips and Potatoes

Preparation time: 10 minutes | Cook time: 20 minutes | Serves 4

✧ Oil, for spraying

✧ 227 g baby potatoes, cut in half

✧ ½ teaspoon salt

✧ 450 g steak, cut into ½-inch pieces

✧ 1 teaspoon Worcester sauce

✧ 1 teaspoon garlic powder

✧ ½ teaspoon salt

✧ ½ teaspoon ground black pepper

Instructions

1. Line the air fryer basket with parchment and spray lightly with oil. 2.In a microwave-safe bowl, combine the potatoes and salt, then pour in about ½ inch of water. 3.Microwave for 7 minutes, or until the potatoes are nearly tender. Drain. 4.In a large bowl, gently mix together the steak, potatoes, Worcester sauce, garlic, salt, and black pepper. 5.Spread the mixture in an even layer in the prepared basket. Air fry at 200°C for 12 to 17 minutes, stirring after 5 to 6 minutes. 6.The cooking time will depend on the thickness of the meat and preferred doneness.

Churro Bites

Preparation time: 5 minutes | Cook time: 6 minutes | Makes 36 bites

- ✧ Oil, for spraying
- ✧ 1 (500 g) package frozen puffed pastry, thawed
- ✧ 180 g caster sugar
- ✧ 1 tablespoon ground cinnamon
- ✧ 90 g icing sugar
- ✧ 1 tablespoon milk

Instructions

1. Preheat the air fryer to 200°C. 2.Line the air fryer basket with parchment and spray lightly with oil. 3.Unfold the puff pastry onto a clean work surface. Using a sharp knife, cut the dough into 36 bite-size pieces. 4.Place the dough pieces in one layer in the prepared basket, taking care not to let the pieces touch or overlap. 5.Cook for 3 minutes, flip, and cook for another 3 minutes, or until puffed and golden. In a small bowl, mix together the caster sugar and cinnamon. 6.In another small bowl, whisk together the icing sugar and milk. 7.Dredge the bites in the cinnamon-sugar mixture until evenly coated. 8.Serve with the icing on the side for dipping.

Berry Cheese cake

Preparation time: 5 minutes | Cook time: 10 minutes | Serves 4

- ✧ Oil, for spraying
- ✧ 227 g soft white cheese
- ✧ 6 tablespoons sugar
- ✧ 1 tablespoon sour cream
- ✧ 1 large egg
- ✧ ½ teaspoon vanilla extract
- ✧ ¼ teaspoon lemon juice
- ✧ 120 g fresh mixed berries

Instructions

1. Preheat the air fryer to 180°C. 2.Line the air fryer basket with parchment and spray lightly with oil. 3.In a blender, combine the soft white cheese, sugar, sour cream, egg, vanilla, and lemon juice and blend until smooth. 4.Pour the mixture into a 4-inch springform pan. 5.Place the pan in the prepared basket. Cook for 8 to 10 minutes, or until only the very centre jiggles slightly when the pan is moved. 6.Refrigerate the cheesecake in the pan for at least 2 hours. 7.Release the sides from the springform pan, top the cheesecake with the mixed berries, and serve.

Air Fried Tortilla Chips

Preparation time: 5 minutes | Cook time: 10 minutes | Serves 4

- ✧ 4 six-inch corn tortillas, cut in half and slice into thirds
- ✧ 1 tablespoon rapeseed oil
- ✧ ¼ teaspoon rock salt
- ✧ Cooking spray

Instructions

1. Preheat the air fryer to 180°C. 2.Spritz the air fryer basket with cooking spray. 3.On a clean work surface, brush the tortilla chips with rapeseed oil, then transfer the chips in the preheated air fryer. 4.Air fry for 10 minutes or until crunchy and lightly browned. 5.Shake the basket and sprinkle with salt halfway through the cooking time. 6.Transfer the chips onto a plate lined with paper towels. 7.Serve immediately.

Sweet Maize and Carrot Fritters

Preparation time: 10 minutes | Cook time: 8 to 11 minutes | Serves 4

- ✧ 1 medium-sized carrot, grated
- ✧ 1 brown onion, finely chopped
- ✧ 4 ounces (113 g) canned sweet maize kernels, drained
- ✧ 1 teaspoon sea salt flakes
- ✧ 1 tablespoon chopped fresh coriander
- ✧ 1 medium-sized egg, whisked
- ✧ 2 tablespoons plain milk
- ✧ 1 cup grated Parmesan cheese
- ✧ ¼ cup flour
- ✧ ⅓ teaspoon baking powder
- ✧ ⅓ teaspoon sugar
- ✧ Cooking spray

Instructions

1. Preheat the air fryer to 350°F (177°C). 2. Place the grated carrot in a colander and press down to squeeze out any excess moisture. Dry it with a paper towel. 3. Combine the carrots with the remaining ingredients. 4. Mold 1 tablespoon of the mixture into a ball and press it down with your hand or a spoon to flatten it. Repeat until the rest of the mixture is used up. 5. Spritz the balls with cooking spray. 6. Arrange in the air fryer basket, taking care not to overlap any balls. Bake for 8 to 11 minutes, or until they're firm. 7. Serve warm.

Peppery Brown Rice Fritters

Preparation time: 10 minutes | Cook time: 8 to 10 minutes | Serves 4

- ✧ 1 (284 g) bag frozen cooked brown rice, thawed
- ✧ 1 egg
- ✧ 3 tablespoons brown rice flour
- ✧ 80 g finely grated carrots
- ✧ 80 g minced red pepper
- ✧ 2 tablespoons minced fresh basil
- ✧ 3 tablespoons grated Parmesan cheese
- ✧ 2 teaspoons olive oil

Instructions

1. Preheat the air fryer to 190°C. 2.In a small bowl, combine the thawed rice, egg, and flour and mix to blend. 3.Stir in the carrots, pepper, basil, and Parmesan cheese. 4.Form the mixture into 8 fritters and drizzle with the olive oil. 5.Put the fritters carefully into the air fryer basket. 6.Air fry for 8 to 10 minutes, or until the fritters are golden brown and cooked through. 7.Serve immediately.

Purple Potato Chips with Rosemary

Preparation time: 10 minutes | Cook time: 9 to 14 minutes | Serves 6

- ✧ 235 ml Greek yoghurt

- ◇ 2 chipotle chillies, minced
- ◇ 2 tablespoons adobo or chipotle sauce
- ◇ 1 teaspoon paprika
- ◇ 1 tablespoon lemon juice
- ◇ 10 purple fingerling or miniature potatoes
- ◇ 1 teaspoon olive oil
- ◇ 2 teaspoons minced fresh rosemary leaves
- ◇ ⅛ teaspoon cayenne pepper
- ◇ ¼ teaspoon coarse sea salt

Instructions

1. Preheat the air fryer to 200°C. 2.In a medium bowl, combine the yoghurt, minced chillies, adobo sauce, paprika, and lemon juice. Mix well and refrigerate. 3.Wash the potatoes and dry them with paper towels. 4.Slice the potatoes lengthwise, as thinly as possible. You tin use a mandoline, a vegetable peeler, or a very sharp knife. 5.Combine the potato slices in a medium bowl and drizzle with the olive oil; toss to coat. 6.Air fry the chips, in batches, in the air fryer basket, for 9 to 14 minutes. 7.Use tongs to gently rearrange the chips halfway during cooking time. 8.Sprinkle the chips with the rosemary, cayenne pepper, and sea salt. 9.Serve with the chipotle sauce for dipping.

Traditional Queso Fundido

Preparation time: 10 minutes | Cook time: 25 minutes | Serves 4

- ◇ 110 g fresh Mexican (or Spanish if unavailable) chorizo, casings removed
- ◇ 1 medium onion, chopped
- ◇ 3 cloves garlic, minced
- ◇ 235 g chopped tomato
- ◇ 2 jalapeños, deseeded and diced
- ◇ 2 teaspoons ground cumin
- ◇ 475 g shredded Oaxaca or Mozzarella cheese
- ◇ 120 ml half-and-half (60 g whole milk and 60 ml cream combined)
- ◇ Celery sticks or tortilla chips, for serving

Instructions

1. Preheat the air fryer to 200°C. 2.In a baking tray, combine the chorizo, onion, garlic, tomato, jalapeños, and cumin. Stir to combine. 3.Place the pan in the air fryer basket. 4.Air fry for 15 minutes, or until the banger is cooked, stirring halfway through the cooking time to break up the banger. 5.Add the cheese and half-and-half; stir to combine. 6.Air fry for 10 minutes, or until the cheese has melted. 7.Serve with celery sticks or maize wrap chips.

Spinach and Carrot Balls

Preparation time: 10 minutes | Cook time: 10 minutes | Serves 4

- ◇ 2 slices toasted bread
- ◇ 1 carrot, peeled and grated
- ◇ 1 package fresh spinach, blanched and chopped
- ◇ ½ onion, chopped
- ◇ 1 egg, beaten
- ◇ ½ teaspoon garlic powder
- ◇ 1 teaspoon minced garlic
- ◇ 1 teaspoon salt
- ◇ ½ teaspoon black pepper
- ◇ 1 tablespoon Engevita yeast flakes
- ◇ 1 tablespoon flour

Instructions

1. Preheat the air fryer to 200°C. 2.In a food processor, pulse the toasted bread to form breadcrumbs. 3.Transfer into a shallow dish or bowl. In a bowl, mix together all the other ingredients. 4.Use your hands to shape the mixture into small-sized balls. 5.Roll the balls in the breadcrumbs, ensuring to cover them well. 6.Put in the air fryer basket and air fry for 10 minutes. 7.Serve immediately.

Air Fried Courgette Sticks

Preparation time: 5 minutes | Cook time: 20 minutes | Serves 4

- ◇ 1 medium courgette, cut into 48 sticks
- ◇ 30 g seasoned breadcrumbs

- ✧ 1 tablespoon melted margarine
- ✧ Cooking spray

Instructions

1. Preheat the air fryer to 180ºC. Spritz the air fryer basket with cooking spray and set aside. In 2 different shallow bowls, add the seasoned breadcrumbs and the margarine. One by one, dredge the courgette sticks into the margarine, then roll in the breadcrumbs to coat evenly. Arrange the crusted sticks on a plate. Place the courgette sticks in the prepared air fryer basket. Work in two batches to avoid overcrowding. Air fry for 10 minutes, or until golden brown and crispy. Shake the basket halfway through to cook evenly. When the cooking time is over, transfer the fries to a wire rack. Rest for 5 minutes and serve warm.

Crunchy Fried Okra

Preparation time: 5 minutes | Cook time: 8 to 10 minutes | Serves 4

- ✧ 120 g self-raising yellow cornmeal (alternatively add 1 tablespoon baking powder to cornmeal)
- ✧ 1 teaspoon Italian-style seasoning
- ✧ 1 teaspoon paprika
- ✧ 1 teaspoon salt
- ✧ ½ teaspoon freshly ground black pepper
- ✧ 2 large eggs, beaten
- ✧ 475 g okra slices
- ✧ Cooking spray

Instructions

1. Preheat the air fryer to 200ºC. 2.Line the air fryer basket with parchment paper. In a shallow bowl, whisk the cornmeal, Italian-style seasoning, paprika, salt, and pepper until blended. 3.Place the beaten eggs in a second shallow bowl. Add the okra to the beaten egg and stir to coat. 4.Add the egg and okra mixture to the cornmeal mixture and stir until coated. 5.Place the okra on the parchment and spritz it with oil. 6.Air fry for 4 minutes. Shake the basket, spritz the okra with oil, and air fry for 4 to 6 minutes more until lightly browned and crispy. 7.Serve immediately.

Easy Cajun Chicken Drumsticks

Preparation time: 5 minutes | Cook time: 40 minutes | Serves 5

- ✧ 1 tablespoon olive oil
- ✧ 10 chicken drumsticks
- ✧ 1½ tablespoons Cajun seasoning
- ✧ Salt and ground black pepper, to taste

Instructions

1. Preheat the air fryer to 200°C. Grease the air fryer basket with olive oil. 2. On a clean work surface, rub the chicken drumsticks with Cajun seasoning, salt, and ground black pepper. 3. Arrange the seasoned chicken drumsticks in a single layer in the air fryer. You need to work in batches to avoid overcrowding. 4. Air fry for 18 minutes or until lightly browned. Flip the drumsticks halfway through. 5. Remove the chicken drumsticks from the air fryer. Serve immediately.

Sriracha-Honey Chicken Nuggets

Preparation time: 15 minutes | Cook time: 19 minutes | Serves 6

- ✧ Oil, for spraying
- ✧ 1 large egg
- ✧ 180 ml milk
- ✧ 65 g plain flour
- ✧ 2 tablespoons icing sugar
- ✧ ½ teaspoon paprika
- ✧ ½ teaspoon salt
- ✧ ½ teaspoon freshly ground black pepper
- ✧ 2 boneless, skinless chicken breasts, cut into bite-size pieces
- ✧ 140 g barbecue sauce
- ✧ 2 tablespoons honey
- ✧ 1 tablespoon Sriracha

Instructions

1. Line the air fryer basket with parchment and spray lightly with oil. 2. In a small bowl, whisk together the egg and milk. 3. In a medium bowl, combine the flour, icing sugar, paprika, salt, and black pepper and stir. 4. Coat the chicken in the egg mixture, then dredge in the flour mixture until evenly coated. 5. Place the chicken in the prepared basket and spray liberally with oil. 6. Air fry at 200°C for 8 minutes, flip, spray with more oil, and cook for another 6 to 8 minutes, or until the internal temperature reaches 76°C and the juices run clear. 7. In a large bowl, mix together the barbecue sauce, honey, and Sriracha. 8. Transfer the chicken to the bowl and toss until well coated with the barbecue sauce mixture. 9. Line the air fryer basket with fresh parchment, return the chicken to the basket, and cook for another 2 to 3 minutes, until browned and crispy.

Garlic Dill Wings

Preparation time: 5 minutes | Cook time: 25 minutes | Serves 4

- ✧ 900 g bone-in chicken wings, separated at joints
- ✧ ½ teaspoon salt
- ✧ ½ teaspoon ground black pepper
- ✧ ½ teaspoon onion powder
- ✧ ½ teaspoon garlic powder
- ✧ 1 teaspoon dried dill

Instructions

1. In a large bowl, toss wings with salt, pepper, onion powder, garlic powder, and dill until evenly coated. Place wings into ungreased air fryer basket in a single layer, working in batches if needed. 2. Adjust the temperature to 200°C and air fry for 25 minutes, shaking the basket every 7 minutes during cooking. Wings should have an internal temperature of at least 76°C and be

golden brown when done. Serve warm.

Chicken with Pineapple and Peach

Preparation time: 10 minutes | Cook time: 14 to 15 minutes | Serves 4

- ✧ 1 (450 g) low-sodium boneless, skinless chicken breasts, cut into 1-inch pieces
- ✧ 1 medium red onion, chopped
- ✧ 1 (230 g) tin pineapple chunks, drained, 60 ml juice reserved
- ✧ 1 tablespoon peanut oil or safflower oil
- ✧ 1 peach, peeled, pitted, and cubed
- ✧ 1 tablespoon cornflour
- ✧ ½ teaspoon ground ginger
- ✧ ¼ teaspoon ground allspice
- ✧ Brown rice, cooked (optional)

Instructions

1. Preheat the air fryer to 196°C. 2. In a medium metal bowl, mix the chicken, red onion, pineapple, and peanut oil. Bake in the air fryer for 9 minutes. Remove and stir. 3. Add the peach and return the bowl to the air fryer. Bake for 3 minutes more. Remove and stir again. 4. In a small bowl, whisk the reserved pineapple juice, the cornflour, ginger, and allspice well. Add to the chicken mixture and stir to combine. 5. Bake for 2 to 3 minutes more, or until the chicken reaches an internal temperature of 76°C on a meat thermometer and the sauce is slightly thickened. 6. Serve immediately over hot cooked brown rice, if desired.

Sesame Chicken Breast

Preparation time: 10 minutes | Cook time: 18 minutes | Serves 6

- ✧ Oil, for spraying
- ✧ 2 (170 g) boneless, skinless chicken breasts, cut into bite-size pieces
- ✧ 30 g cornflour plus 1 tablespoon
- ✧ 60 ml soy sauce
- ✧ 2 tablespoons packed light brown sugar
- ✧ 2 tablespoons pineapple juice
- ✧ 1 tablespoon black treacle
- ✧ ½ teaspoon ground ginger
- ✧ 1 tablespoon water
- ✧ 2 teaspoons sesame seeds

Instructions

1. Line the air fryer basket with parchment and spray lightly with oil. 2. Place the chicken and 60 g of cornflour in a zip-top plastic bag, seal, and shake well until evenly coated. 3. Place the chicken in an even layer in the prepared basket and spray liberally with oil. You may need to work in batches, depending on the size of your fryer. 4. Air fry at 200°C for 9 minutes, flip, spray with more oil, and cook for another 8 to 9 minutes, or until the internal temperature reaches 76°C. 5. In a small saucepan, combine the soy sauce, brown sugar, pineapple juice, black treacle, and ginger over medium heat and cook, stirring frequently, until the brown sugar has dissolved. 6. In a small bowl, mix together the water and remaining 1 tablespoon of cornflour. Pour it into the soy sauce mixture. 7. Bring the mixture to a boil, stirring frequently, until the sauce thickens. Remove from the heat. 8. Transfer the chicken to a large bowl, add the sauce, and toss until evenly coated. Sprinkle with the sesame seeds and serve.

Chicken Paillard

Preparation time: 10 minutes | Cook time: 10 minutes | Serves 2

- ✧ 2 large eggs, room temperature
- ✧ 1 tablespoon water
- ✧ 20 g powdered Parmesan cheese or pork dust
- ✧ 2 teaspoons dried thyme leaves
- ✧ 1 teaspoon ground black pepper
- ✧ 2 (140 g) boneless, skinless chicken breasts, pounded to ½ inch thick
- ✧ Lemon Butter Sauce:
- ✧ 2 tablespoons unsalted butter, melted
- ✧ 2 teaspoons lemon juice

- ✧ ¼ teaspoon finely chopped fresh thyme leaves, plus more for garnish
- ✧ ⅛ teaspoon fine sea salt
- ✧ Lemon slices, for serving

Instructions

1. Spray the air fryer basket with avocado oil. Preheat the air fryer to 200°C. 2. Beat the eggs in a shallow dish, then add the water and stir well. 3. In a separate shallow dish, mix together the Parmesan, thyme, and pepper until well combined. 4. One at a time, dip the chicken breasts in the eggs and let any excess drip off, then dredge both sides of the chicken in the Parmesan mixture. As you finish, set the coated chicken in the air fryer basket. 5. Roast the chicken in the air fryer for 5 minutes, then flip the chicken and cook for another 5 minutes, or until cooked through and the internal temperature reaches 76°C. 6. While the chicken cooks, make the lemon butter sauce: In a small bowl, mix together all the sauce ingredients until well combined. 7. Plate the chicken and pour the sauce over it. Garnish with chopped fresh thyme and serve with lemon slices. 8. Store leftovers in an airtight container in the refrigerator for up to 4 days. Reheat in a preheated 200°C air fryer for 5 minutes, or until heated through.

Peanut Butter Chicken Satay

Preparation time: 12 minutes | Cook time: 12 to 18 minutes | Serves 4

- ✧ 120 g crunchy peanut butter
- ✧ 80 ml chicken broth
- ✧ 3 tablespoons low-sodium soy sauce
- ✧ 2 tablespoons freshly squeezed lemon juice
- ✧ 2 garlic cloves, minced
- ✧ 2 tablespoons extra-virgin olive oil
- ✧ 1 teaspoon curry powder
- ✧ 450 g chicken tenders
- ✧ Cooking oil spray

Instructions

1. In a medium bowl, whisk the peanut butter, broth, soy sauce, lemon juice, garlic, olive oil, and curry powder until smooth. 2. Place 2 tablespoons of this mixture into a small bowl. Transfer the remaining sauce to a serving bowl and set aside. 3. Add the chicken tenders to the bowl with the 2 tablespoons of sauce and stir to coat. Let stand for a few minutes to marinate. 4. Insert the crisper plate into the basket and the basket into the unit. Preheat the unit by selecting AIR FRY, setting the temperature to 200°C, and setting the time to 3 minutes. Select START/STOP to begin. 5. Run a 6-inch bamboo skewer lengthwise through each chicken tender. 6. Once the unit is preheated, spray the crisper plate with cooking oil. Working in batches, place half the chicken skewers into the basket in a single layer without overlapping. 7. Select AIR FRY, set the temperature to 200°C, and set the time to 9 minutes. Select START/STOP to begin. 8. After 6 minutes, check the chicken. If a food thermometer inserted into the chicken registers 76°C, it is done. If not, resume cooking. 9. Repeat steps 6, 7, and 8 with the remaining chicken. 10. When the cooking is complete, serve the chicken with the reserved sauce.

Easy Chicken Fingers

Preparation time: 20 minutes | Cook time: 30 minutes | Makes 12 chicken fingers

- ✧ 30 g plain flour
- ✧ 120 g panko breadcrumbs
- ✧ 2 tablespoons rapeseed oil
- ✧ 1 large egg
- ✧ 3 boneless and skinless chicken breasts, each cut into 4 strips
- ✧ Coarse salt and freshly ground black pepper, to taste
- ✧ Cooking spray

Instructions

1. Preheat the air fryer to 180°C. Spritz the

air fryer basket with cooking spray. 2. Pour the flour in a large bowl. Combine the panko and rapeseed oil on a shallow dish. Whisk the egg in a separate bowl. 3. Rub the chicken strips with salt and ground black pepper on a clean work surface, then dip the chicken in the bowl of flour. Shake the excess off and dunk the chicken strips in the bowl of whisked egg, then roll the strips over the panko to coat well. 4. Arrange 4 strips in the air fryer basket each time and air fry for 10 minutes or until crunchy and lightly browned. Flip the strips halfway through. Repeat with remaining ingredients. 5. Serve immediately.

Lemon Chicken with Garlic

Preparation time: 5 minutes | Cook time: 20 to 25 minutes | Serves 4

- ✧ 8 bone-in chicken thighs, skin on
- ✧ 1 tablespoon olive oil
- ✧ 1½ teaspoons lemon-pepper seasoning
- ✧ ½ teaspoon paprika
- ✧ ½ teaspoon garlic powder
- ✧ ¼ teaspoon freshly ground black pepper
- ✧ Juice of ½ lemon

Instructions

1. Preheat the air fryer to 180°C. 2. Place the chicken in a large bowl and drizzle with the olive oil. Top with the lemon-pepper seasoning, paprika, garlic powder, and freshly ground black pepper. Toss until thoroughly coated. 3. Working in batches if necessary, arrange the chicken in a single layer in the basket of the air fryer. Pausing halfway through the cooking time to turn the chicken, air fry for 20 to 25 minutes, until a thermometer inserted into the thickest piece registers 76°C. 4. Transfer the chicken to a serving platter and squeeze the lemon juice over the top.

Pecan Turkey Cutlets

Preparation time: 10 minutes | Cook time: 10 to 12 minutes per batch |

Serves 4

- ✧ 45 g panko bread crumbs
- ✧ ¼ teaspoon salt
- ✧ ¼ teaspoon pepper
- ✧ ¼ teaspoon mustard powder
- ✧ ¼ teaspoon poultry seasoning
- ✧ 50 g pecans
- ✧ 15 g cornflour
- ✧ 1 egg, beaten
- ✧ 450 g turkey cutlets, ½-inch thick
- ✧ Salt and pepper, to taste
- ✧ Oil for misting or cooking spray

Instructions

1. Place the panko crumbs, ¼ teaspoon salt, ¼ teaspoon pepper, mustard, and poultry seasoning in food processor. Process until crumbs are finely crushed. Add pecans and process in short pulses just until nuts are finely chopped. Go easy so you don't overdo it! 2. Preheat the air fryer to 180°C. 3. Place cornflour in one shallow dish and beaten egg in another. Transfer coating mixture from food processor into a third shallow dish. 4. Sprinkle turkey cutlets with salt and pepper to taste. 5. Dip cutlets in cornflour and shake off excess. Then dip in beaten egg and roll in crumbs, pressing to coat well. Spray both sides with oil or cooking spray. 6. Place 2 cutlets in air fryer basket in a single layer and cook for 10 to 12 minutes or until juices run clear. 7. Repeat step 6 to cook remaining cutlets.

Nacho Chicken Fries

Preparation time: 20 minutes | Cook time: 6 to 7 minutes per batch | Serves 4 to 6

- ✧ 450 g chicken tenders
- ✧ Salt, to taste
- ✧ 15 g flour
- ✧ 2 eggs
- ✧ 45 g panko bread crumbs
- ✧ 20 g crushed organic nacho cheese maize wrap chips

- ◇ Oil for misting or cooking spray
- ◇ Seasoning Mix:
- ◇ 1 tablespoon chilli powder
- ◇ 1 teaspoon ground cumin
- ◇ ½ teaspoon garlic powder
- ◇ ½ teaspoon onion powder

Instructions

1. Stir together all seasonings in a small cup and set aside. 2. Cut chicken tenders in half crosswise, then cut into strips no wider than about ½ inch. 3. Preheat the air fryer to 200°C. 4. Salt chicken to taste. Place strips in large bowl and sprinkle with 1 tablespoon of the seasoning mix. Stir well to distribute seasonings. 5. Add flour to chicken and stir well to coat all sides. 6. Beat eggs together in a shallow dish. 7. In a second shallow dish, combine the panko, crushed chips, and the remaining 2 teaspoons of seasoning mix. 8. Dip chicken strips in eggs, then roll in crumbs. Mist with oil or cooking spray. 9. Chicken strips will cook best if done in two batches. They tin be crowded and overlapping a little but not stacked in double or triple layers. 10. Cook for 4 minutes. Shake basket, mist with oil, and cook 2 to 3 more minutes, until chicken juices run clear and outside is crispy. 1Instructions

1. Repeat step 10 to cook remaining chicken fries.

Curried Orange Honey Chicken

Preparation time: 10 minutes | Cook time: 16 to 19 minutes | Serves 4

- ◇ 340 g boneless, skinless chicken thighs, cut into 1-inch pieces
- ◇ 1 yellow pepper, cut into 1½-inch pieces
- ◇ 1 small red onion, sliced
- ◇ Olive oil for misting
- ◇ 60 ml chicken stock
- ◇ 2 tablespoons honey
- ◇ 60 ml orange juice
- ◇ 1 tablespoon cornflour
- ◇ 2 to 3 teaspoons curry powder

Instructions

1. Preheat the air fryer to 190°C. 2. Put the chicken thighs, pepper, and red onion in the air fryer basket and mist with olive oil. 3. Roast for 12 to 14 minutes or until the chicken is cooked to 76°C, shaking the basket halfway through cooking time. 4. Remove the chicken and vegetables from the air fryer basket and set aside. 5. In a metal bowl, combine the stock, honey, orange juice, cornflour, and curry powder, and mix well. Add the chicken and vegetables, stir, and put the bowl in the basket. 6. Return the basket to the air fryer and roast for 2 minutes. Remove and stir, then roast for 2 to 3 minutes or until the sauce is thickened and bubbly. 7. Serve warm.

Chicken and Broccoli Casserole

Preparation time: 5 minutes | Cook time: 20 to 25 minutes | Serves 4

- ◇ 230 g broccoli, chopped into florets
- ◇ 280 g shredded cooked chicken
- ◇ 115 g cream cheese
- ◇ 80 g double cream
- ◇ 1½ teaspoons Dijon mustard
- ◇ ½ teaspoon garlic powder
- ◇ Salt and freshly ground black pepper, to taste
- ◇ 2 tablespoons chopped fresh basil
- ◇ 230 g shredded Cheddar cheese

Instructions

1. Preheat the air fryer to 200°C. Lightly coat a casserole dish that will fit in air fryer, with olive oil and set aside. 2. Place the broccoli in a large glass bowl with 1 tablespoon of water and cover with a microwavable plate. Microwave on high for 2 to 3 minutes until the broccoli is bright green but not mushy. Drain if necessary and add to another large bowl along with the shredded chicken. 3. In the same glass bowl used to microwave the broccoli, combine the cream cheese and cream. Microwave for 30 seconds to 1 minute

on high and stir until smooth. Add the mustard and garlic powder and season to taste with salt and freshly ground black pepper. Whisk until the sauce is smooth. 4. Pour the warm sauce over the broccoli and chicken mixture and then add the basil. Using a silicone spatula, gently fold the mixture until thoroughly combined. 5. Transfer the chicken mixture to the prepared casserole dish and top with the cheese. Air fry for 20 to 25 minutes until warmed through and the cheese has browned.

Herb-Buttermilk Chicken Breast

Preparation time: 5 minutes | Cook time: 40 minutes | Serves 2

- ✧ 1 large bone-in, skin-on chicken breast
- ✧ 240 ml buttermilk
- ✧ 1½ teaspoons dried parsley
- ✧ 1½ teaspoons dried chives
- ✧ ¾ teaspoon kosher salt
- ✧ ½ teaspoon dried dill
- ✧ ½ teaspoon onion powder
- ✧ ¼ teaspoon garlic powder
- ✧ ¼ teaspoon dried tarragon
- ✧ Cooking spray

Instructions

1. Place the chicken breast in a bowl and pour over the buttermilk, turning the chicken in it to make sure it's completely covered. Let the chicken stand at room temperature for at least 20 minutes or in the refrigerator for up to 4 hours. 2. Meanwhile, in a bowl, stir together the parsley, chives, salt, dill, onion powder, garlic powder, and tarragon. 3. Preheat the air fryer to 150°C. 4. Remove the chicken from the buttermilk, letting the excess drip off, then place the chicken skin-side up directly in the air fryer. Sprinkle the seasoning mix all over the top of the chicken breast, then let stand until the herb mix soaks into the buttermilk, at least 5 minutes. 5. Spray the top of the chicken with cooking spray. Bake for 10 minutes, then

increase the temperature to 180°C and bake until an instant-read thermometer inserted into the thickest part of the breast reads 80°C and the chicken is deep golden brown, 30 to 35 minutes. 6. Transfer the chicken breast to a cutting board, let rest for 10 minutes, then cut the meat off the bone and cut into thick slices for serving.

French Garlic Chicken

Preparation time: 30 minutes | Cook time: 27 minutes | Serves 4

- ✧ 2 tablespoon extra-virgin olive oil
- ✧ 1 tablespoon Dijon mustard
- ✧ 1 tablespoon apple cider vinegar
- ✧ 3 cloves garlic, minced
- ✧ 2 teaspoons herbes de Provence
- ✧ ½ teaspoon kosher salt
- ✧ 1 teaspoon black pepper
- ✧ 450 g boneless, skinless chicken thighs, halved crosswise
- ✧ 2 tablespoons butter
- ✧ 8 cloves garlic, chopped
- ✧ 60 g heavy whipping cream

Instructions

1. In a small bowl, combine the olive oil, mustard, vinegar, minced garlic, herbes de Provence, salt, and pepper. Use a wire whisk to emulsify the mixture. 2. Pierce the chicken all over with a fork to allow the marinade to penetrate better. Place the chicken in a resealable plastic bag, pour the marinade over, and seal. Massage until the chicken is well coated. Marinate at room temperature for 30 minutes or in the refrigerator for up to 24 hours. 3. When you are ready to cook, place the butter and chopped garlic in a baking pan and place it in the air fryer basket. Set the air fryer to 200°C for 5 minutes, or until the butter has melted and the garlic is sizzling. 4. Add the chicken and the marinade to the seasoned butter. Set the air fryer to 180°C for 15 minutes. Use a meat thermometer to ensure the chicken has

reached an internal temperature of 76°C. Transfer the chicken to a plate and cover lightly with foil to keep warm. 5. Add the cream to the pan, stirring to combine with the garlic, butter, and cooking juices. Place the pan in the air fryer basket. Set the air fryer to 180°C for 7 minutes. 6. Pour the thickened sauce over the chicken and serve.

Porchetta-Style Chicken Breasts

Preparation time: 10 minutes | Cook time: 15 minutes | Serves 4

- ✧ 25 g fresh parsley leaves
- ✧ 10 g roughly chopped fresh chives
- ✧ 4 cloves garlic, peeled
- ✧ 2 tablespoons lemon juice
- ✧ 3 teaspoons fine sea salt
- ✧ 1 teaspoon dried rubbed sage
- ✧ 1 teaspoon fresh rosemary leaves
- ✧ 1 teaspoon ground fennel
- ✧ ½ teaspoon red pepper flakes
- ✧ 4 (115 g) boneless, skinless chicken breasts, pounded to ¼ inch thick
- ✧ 8 slices bacon
- ✧ Sprigs of fresh rosemary, for garnish (optional)

Instructions

1. Spray the air fryer basket with avocado oil. Preheat the air fryer to 170°C. 2. Place the parsley, chives, garlic, lemon juice, salt, sage, rosemary, fennel, and red pepper flakes in a food processor and purée until a smooth paste forms. 3. Place the chicken breasts on a cutting board and rub the paste all over the tops. With a short end facing you, roll each breast up like a jelly roll to make a log and secure it with toothpicks. 4. Wrap 2 slices of bacon around each chicken breast log to cover the entire breast. Secure the bacon with toothpicks. 5. Place the chicken breast logs in the air fryer basket and air fry for 5 minutes, flip the logs over, and cook for another 5 minutes. Increase the heat to 200°C and cook until the bacon is crisp, about 5 minutes

more. 6. Remove the toothpicks and garnish with fresh rosemary sprigs, if desired, before serving. Store leftovers in an airtight container in the refrigerator for up to 4 days or in the freezer for up to a month. Reheat in a preheated 180°C air fryer for 5 minutes, then increase the heat to 200°C and cook for 2 minutes to crisp the bacon.

Spice-Rubbed Chicken Thighs

Preparation time: 10 minutes | Cook time: 25 minutes | Serves 4

- ✧ 4 (115 g) bone-in, skin-on chicken thighs
- ✧ ½ teaspoon salt
- ✧ ½ teaspoon garlic powder
- ✧ 2 teaspoons chilli powder
- ✧ 1 teaspoon paprika
- ✧ 1 teaspoon ground cumin
- ✧ 1 small lime, halved

Instructions

1. Pat chicken thighs dry and sprinkle with salt, garlic powder, chilli powder, paprika, and cumin. 2. Squeeze juice from ½ lime over thighs. Place thighs into ungreased air fryer basket. Adjust the temperature to 190°C and roast for 25 minutes, turning thighs halfway through cooking. Thighs will be crispy and browned with an internal temperature of at least 76°C when done. 3. Transfer thighs to a large serving plate and drizzle with remaining lime juice. Serve warm.

Pecan-Crusted Chicken Tenders

Preparation time: 10 minutes | Cook time: 12 minutes | Serves 4

- ✧ 2 tablespoons mayonnaise
- ✧ 1 teaspoon Dijon mustard
- ✧ 455 g boneless, skinless chicken tenders
- ✧ ½ teaspoon salt
- ✧ ¼ teaspoon ground black pepper
- ✧ 75 g chopped roasted pecans, finely ground

Instructions

1. In a small bowl, whisk mayonnaise and mustard until combined. Brush mixture onto chicken tenders on both sides, then sprinkle tenders with salt and pepper. 2. Place pecans in a medium bowl and press each tender into pecans to coat each side. 3. Place tenders into ungreased air fryer basket in a single layer, working in batches if needed. Adjust the temperature to (190°C and roast for 12 minutes, turning tenders halfway through cooking. Tenders will be golden brown and have an internal temperature of at least 76°C when done. Serve warm.

Nashville Hot Chicken

Preparation time: 20 minutes | Cook time: 24 to 28 minutes | Serves 8

Instructions

1.4 kg bone-in, skin-on chicken pieces, breasts halved crosswise

- ✧ 1 tablespoon sea salt
- ✧ 1 tablespoon freshly ground black pepper
- ✧ 70 g finely ground blanched almond flour
- ✧ 130 g grated Parmesan cheese
- ✧ 1 tablespoon baking powder
- ✧ 2 teaspoons garlic powder, divided
- ✧ 120 g heavy (whipping) cream
- ✧ 2 large eggs, beaten
- ✧ 1 tablespoon vinegar-based hot sauce
- ✧ Avocado oil spray
- ✧ 115 g unsalted butter
- ✧ 120 ml avocado oil
- ✧ 1 tablespoon cayenne pepper (more or less to taste)
- ✧ 2 tablespoons Xylitol

Instructions

1. Sprinkle the chicken with the salt and pepper. 2. In a large shallow bowl, whisk together the almond flour, Parmesan cheese, baking powder, and 1 teaspoon of the garlic powder. 3. In a separate bowl, whisk together the double cream, eggs, and hot sauce. 4. Dip the chicken pieces in the egg, then coat each with the almond flour mixture, pressing the mixture into the chicken to adhere. Allow to sit for 15 minutes to let the breading set. 5. Set the air fryer to 200°C. Place the chicken in a single layer in the air fryer basket, being careful not to overcrowd the pieces, working in batches if necessary. Spray the chicken with oil and roast for 13 minutes. 6. Carefully flip the chicken and spray it with more oil. Reduce the air fryer temperature to 180°C. Roast for another 11 to 15 minutes, until an instant-read thermometer reads 70°C. 7. While the chicken cooks, heat the butter, avocado oil, cayenne pepper, xylitol, and remaining 1 teaspoon of garlic powder in a saucepan over medium-low heat. Cook until the butter is melted and the sugar substitute has dissolved. 8. Remove the chicken from the air fryer. Use tongs to dip the chicken in the sauce. Place the coated chicken on a rack over a baking sheet, and allow it to rest for 5 minutes before serving.

Broccoli and Cheese Stuffed Chicken

Preparation time: 15 minutes | Cook time: 20 minutes | Serves 4

- ✧ 60 g cream cheese, softened
- ✧ 70 g chopped fresh broccoli, steamed
- ✧ 120 g shredded sharp Cheddar cheese
- ✧ 4 (170 g) boneless, skinless chicken breasts
- ✧ 2 tablespoons mayonnaise
- ✧ ¼ teaspoon salt
- ✧ ¼ teaspoon garlic powder
- ✧ ⅛ teaspoon ground black pepper

Instructions

1. In a medium bowl, combine cream cheese, broccoli, and Cheddar. Cut a 4-inch pocket into each chicken breast. Evenly divide mixture between chicken breasts; stuff the pocket of each chicken breast with the

mixture. 2. Spread ¼ tablespoon mayonnaise per side of each chicken breast, then sprinkle both sides of breasts with salt, garlic powder, and pepper. 3. Place stuffed chicken breasts into ungreased air fryer basket so that the open seams face up. Adjust the temperature to 180°C and air fry for 20 minutes, turning chicken halfway through cooking. When done, chicken will be golden and have an internal temperature of at least 76°C. Serve warm.

Crispy Duck with Cherry Sauce

Preparation time: 10 minutes | Cook time: 33 minutes | Serves 2 to 4

- ✧ 1 whole duck (2.3 kg), split in half, back and rib bones removed
- ✧ 1 teaspoon olive oil
- ✧ Salt and freshly ground black pepper, to taste
- ✧ Cherry Sauce:
- ✧ 1 tablespoon butter
- ✧ 1 shallot, minced
- ✧ 120 ml sherry
- ✧ 240 g cherry preserves
- ✧ 240 ml chicken stock
- ✧ 1 teaspoon white wine vinegar
- ✧ 1 teaspoon fresh thyme leaves
- ✧ Salt and freshly ground black pepper, to taste

Instructions

1. Preheat the air fryer to 200°C. 2. Trim some of the fat from the duck. Rub olive oil on the duck and season with salt and pepper. Place the duck halves in the air fryer basket, breast side up and facing the centre of the basket. 3. Air fry the duck for 20 minutes. Turn the duck over and air fry for another 6 minutes. 4. While duck is air frying, make the cherry sauce. Melt the butter in a large sauté pan. Add the shallot and sauté until it is just starting to brown, about 2 to 3 minutes. Add the sherry and deglaze the pan by scraping up any brown bits from the bottom of the pan. Simmer the liquid for a few minutes, until it has reduced by half. Add the cherry preserves, chicken stock and white wine vinegar. Whisk well to combine all the ingredients. Simmer the sauce until it thickens and coats the back of a spoon, about 5 to 7 minutes. Season with salt and pepper and stir in the fresh thyme leaves. 5. When the air fryer timer goes off, spoon some cherry sauce over the duck and continue to air fry at 200°C for 4 more minutes. Then, turn the duck halves back over so that the breast side is facing up. Spoon more cherry sauce over the top of the duck, covering the skin completely. Air fry for 3 more minutes and then remove the duck to a plate to rest for a few minutes. 6. Serve the duck in halves, or cut each piece in half again for a smaller serving. Spoon any additional sauce over the duck or serve it on the side.

CHAPTER 5 BEEF, PORK, AND LAMB

Green Pepper Cheeseburgers

Preparation time: 5 minutes | Cook time: 30 minutes | Serves 4

✧ 2 green peppers
✧ 680 g 85% lean beef mince
✧ 1 clove garlic, minced
✧ 1 teaspoon salt
✧ ½ teaspoon freshly ground black pepper
✧ 4 slices Cheddar cheese (about 85 g)
✧ 4 large lettuce leaves

Instructions

1. Preheat the air fryer to 200ºC. 2. Arrange the peppers in the basket of the air fryer. Pausing halfway through the cooking time to turn the peppers, air fry for 20 minutes, or until they are softened and beginning to char. Transfer the peppers to a large bowl and cover with a plate. When cool enough to handle, peel off the skin, remove the seeds and stems, and slice into strips. Set aside. 3. Meanwhile, in a large bowl, combine the beef with the garlic, salt, and pepper. Shape the beef into 4 patties. 4. Lower the heat on the air fryer to 180ºC. Arrange the burgers in a single layer in the basket of the air fryer. Pausing halfway through the cooking time to turn the burgers, air fry for 10 minutes, or until a thermometer inserted into the thickest part registers 72ºC. 5. Top the burgers with the cheese slices and continue baking for a minute or two, just until the cheese has melted. Serve the burgers on a lettuce leaf topped with the roasted peppers.

Mustard Lamb Chops

Preparation time: 5 minutes | Cook time: 14 minutes | Serves 4

✧ Oil, for spraying
✧ 1 tablespoon Dijon mustard
✧ 2 teaspoons lemon juice
✧ ½ teaspoon dried tarragon
✧ ¼ teaspoon salt
✧ ¼ teaspoon freshly ground black pepper
✧ 4 (1¼-inch-thick) loin lamb chops

Instructions

1. Preheat the air fryer to 200ºC. Line the air fryer basket with parchment and spray lightly with oil. 2. In a small bowl, mix together the mustard, lemon juice, tarragon, salt, and black pepper. 3. Pat dry the lamb chops with a paper towel. Brush the chops on both sides with the mustard mixture. 4. Place the chops in the prepared basket. You may need to work in batches, depending on the size of your air fryer. 5. Cook for 8 minutes, flip, and cook for another 6 minutes, or until the internal temperature reaches 52ºC for rare, 64ºC for medium-rare, or 68ºC for medium.

Simple Beef Mince with Courgette

Preparation time: 5 minutes | Cook time: 12 minutes | Serves 4

✧ 680 g beef mince
✧ 450 g chopped courgette
✧ 2 tablespoons extra-virgin olive oil
✧ 1 teaspoon dried oregano
✧ 1 teaspoon dried basil
✧ 1 teaspoon dried rosemary
✧ 2 tablespoons fresh chives, chopped

Instructions

1. Preheat the air fryer to 200ºC. 2. In a large bowl, combine all the ingredients, except for the chives, until well blended. 3. Place the beef and courgette mixture in the baking tray. Air fry for 12 minutes, or until the beef is browned and the courgette is tender. 4. Divide the beef and courgette mixture among four serving dishes. Top with fresh chives and serve hot.

Spaghetti Zoodles and Meatballs

Preparation time: 30 minutes | Cook time: 11 to 13 minutes | Serves 6

- ✧ 450 g beef mince
- ✧ 1½ teaspoons sea salt, plus more for seasoning
- ✧ 1 large egg, beaten
- ✧ 1 teaspoon gelatin
- ✧ 180 g Parmesan cheese
- ✧ 2 teaspoons minced garlic
- ✧ 1 teaspoon Italian seasoning
- ✧ Freshly ground black pepper, to taste
- ✧ Avocado oil spray
- ✧ Keto-friendly marinara sauce, for serving
- ✧ 170 g courgette noodles, made using a spiralizer or store-bought

Instructions

1. Place the beef mince in a large bowl, and season with the salt. 2. Place the egg in a separate bowl and sprinkle with the gelatin. Allow to sit for 5 minutes. 3. Stir the gelatin mixture, then pour it over the ground beef. Add the Parmesan, garlic, and Italian seasoning. Season with salt and pepper. 4. Form the mixture into 1½-inch meatballs and place them on a plate; cover with cling film and refrigerate for at least 1 hour or overnight. 5. Spray the meatballs with oil. Set the air fryer to 200°C and arrange the meatballs in a single layer in the air fryer basket. Air fry for 4 minutes. Flip the meatballs and spray them with more oil. Air fry for 4 minutes more, until an instant-read thermometer reads 72°C. Transfer the meatballs to a plate and allow them to rest. 6. While the meatballs are resting, heat the marinara in a saucepan on the cooker over medium heat. 7. Place the courgette noodles in the air fryer, and cook at 200°C for 3 to 5 minutes. 8. To serve, place the courgette noodles in serving bowls. Top with meatballs and warm marinara.

Vietnamese Grilled Pork

Preparation time: 30 minutes | Cook time: 20 minutes | Serves 6

- ✧ 60 g minced brown onion
- ✧ 2 tablespoons sugar
- ✧ 2 tablespoons vegetable oil
- ✧ 1 tablespoon minced garlic
- ✧ 1 tablespoon fish sauce
- ✧ 1 tablespoon minced fresh lemongrass
- ✧ 2 teaspoons dark soy sauce
- ✧ ½ teaspoon black pepper
- ✧ 680 g boneless pork shoulder, cut into ½-inch-thick slices
- ✧ 60 g chopped salted roasted peanuts
- ✧ 2 tablespoons chopped fresh coriander or parsley

Instructions

1. In a large bowl, combine the onion, sugar, vegetable oil, garlic, fish sauce, lemongrass, soy sauce, and pepper. Add the pork and toss to coat. Marinate at room temperature for 30 minutes, or cover and refrigerate for up to 24 hours. 2. Arrange the pork slices in the air fryer basket; discard the marinade. Set the air fryer to 200°C for 20 minutes, turning the pork halfway through the cooking time. 3. Transfer the pork to a serving platter. Sprinkle with the peanuts and coriander and serve.

BBQ Pork Steaks

Preparation time: 5 minutes | Cook time: 15 minutes | Serves 4

- ✧ 4 pork steaks
- ✧ 1 tablespoon Cajun seasoning
- ✧ 2 tablespoons BBQ sauce
- ✧ 1 tablespoon vinegar
- ✧ 1 teaspoon soy sauce
- ✧ 96 g brown sugar
- ✧ 120 ml ketchup

Instructions

1. Preheat the air fryer to 140°C. 2. Sprinkle pork steaks with Cajun seasoning. 3.

Combine remaining ingredients and brush onto steaks. 4. Add coated steaks to air fryer. Air fry 15 minutes until just browned. 5. Serve immediately.

Pork Loin with Aloha Salsa

Preparation time: 20 minutes | Cook time: 7 to 9 minutes | Serves 4

- ✧ Aloha Salsa:
- ✧ 235 g fresh pineapple, chopped in small pieces
- ✧ 60 g red onion, finely chopped
- ✧ 60 g green or red pepper, chopped
- ✧ ½ teaspoon ground cinnamon
- ✧ 1 teaspoon reduced-salt soy sauce
- ✧ ⅛ teaspoon crushed red pepper
- ✧ ⅛ teaspoon ground black pepper
- ✧ 2 eggs
- ✧ 2 tablespoons milk
- ✧ 30 g flour
- ✧ 30 g panko bread crumbs
- ✧ 4 teaspoons sesame seeds
- ✧ 450 g boneless, thin pork loin or tenderloin (⅜ to ½-inch thick)
- ✧ Pepper and salt
- ✧ 30 g cornflour
- ✧ Oil for misting or cooking spray

Instructions

1. In a medium bowl, stir together all ingredients for salsa. Cover and refrigerate while cooking pork. 2. Preheat the air fryer to 200°C. 3. Beat together eggs and milk in shallow dish. 4. In another shallow dish, mix together the flour, panko, and sesame seeds. 5. Sprinkle pork with pepper and salt to taste. 6. Dip pork in cornflour, egg mixture, and then panko coating. Spray both sides with oil or cooking spray. 7. Cook pork for 3 minutes. Turn pork over, spraying both sides, and continue cooking for 4 to 6 minutes or until well done. 8. Serve fried cutlets with salsa on the side.

Caraway Crusted Beef Steaks

Preparation time: 5 minutes | Cook time: 10 minutes | Serves 4

- ✧ 4 beef steaks
- ✧ 2 teaspoons caraway seeds
- ✧ 2 teaspoons garlic powder
- ✧ Sea salt and cayenne pepper, to taste
- ✧ 1 tablespoon melted butter
- ✧ 40 g almond flour
- ✧ 2 eggs, beaten

Instructions

1. Preheat the air fryer to 180°C. 2. Add the beef steaks to a large bowl and toss with the caraway seeds, garlic powder, salt and pepper until well coated. 3. Stir together the melted butter and almond flour in a bowl. Whisk the eggs in a different bowl. 4. Dredge the seasoned steaks in the eggs, then dip in the almond and butter mixture. 5. Arrange the coated steaks in the air fryer basket. Air fryer for 10 minutes, or until the internal temperature of the beef steaks reaches at least 64°C on a meat thermometer. Flip the steaks once halfway through to ensure even cooking. 6. Transfer the steaks to plates. Let cool for 5 minutes and serve hot.

Spicy Rump Steak

Preparation time: 25 minutes | Cook time: 12 to 18 minutes | Serves 4

- ✧ 2 tablespoons salsa
- ✧ 1 tablespoon minced chipotle pepper or chipotle paste
- ✧ 1 tablespoon apple cider vinegar
- ✧ 1 teaspoon ground cumin
- ✧ ⅛ teaspoon freshly ground black pepper
- ✧ ⅛ teaspoon red pepper flakes
- ✧ 340 g rump steak, cut into 4 pieces and gently pounded to about ⅓ inch thick
- ✧ Cooking oil spray

Instructions

1. In a small bowl, thoroughly mix the salsa, chipotle pepper, vinegar, cumin, black

pepper, and red pepper flakes. Rub this mixture into both sides of each steak piece. Let stand for 15 minutes at room temperature. 2. Insert the crisper plate into the basket and place the basket into the unit. Preheat the unit by selecting AIR FRY, setting the temperature to 200ºC, and setting the time to 3 minutes. Select START/STOP to begin. 3. Once the unit is preheated, spray the crisper plate with cooking oil. Working in batches, place 2 steaks into the basket. 4. Select AIR FRY, set the temperature to 200ºC, and set the time to 9 minutes. Select START/STOP to begin. 5. After about 6 minutes, check the steaks. If a food thermometer inserted into the meat registers at least 64ºC, they are done. If not, resume cooking. 6. When the cooking is done, transfer the steaks to a clean plate and cover with aluminium foil to keep warm. Repeat steps 3, 4, and 5 with the remaining steaks. 7. Thinly slice the steaks against the grain and serve.

Parmesan-Crusted Steak

Preparation time: 30 minutes | Cook time: 12 minutes | Serves 6

- ✧ 120 ml (1 stick) unsalted butter, at room temperature
- ✧ 235 g finely grated Parmesan cheese
- ✧ 30 g finely ground blanched almond flour
- ✧ 680 g sirloin steak
- ✧ Sea salt and freshly ground black pepper, to taste

Instructions

1. Place the butter, Parmesan cheese, and almond flour in a food processor. Process until smooth. Transfer to a sheet of parchment paper and form into a log. Wrap tightly in cling film. Freeze for 45 minutes or refrigerate for at least 4 hours. 2. While the butter is chilling, season the steak liberally with salt and pepper. Let the steak rest at room temperature for about 45 minutes. 3.

Place the grill pan or basket in your air fryer, set it to 200ºC, and let it preheat for 5 minutes. 4. Working in batches, if necessary, place the steak on the grill pan and air fry for 4 minutes. Flip and cook for 3 minutes more, until the steak is brown on both sides. 5. Remove the steak from the air fryer and arrange an equal amount of the Parmesan butter on top of each steak. Return the steak to the air fryer and continue cooking for another 5 minutes, until an instant-read thermometer reads 49ºC for medium-rare and the crust is golden brown (or to your desired doneness). 6. Transfer the cooked steak to a plate; let rest for 10 minutes before serving.

Pork and Tricolor Vegetables Kebabs

Preparation time: 1 hour 20 minutes | Cook time: 8 minutes per batch | Serves 4

- ✧ For the Pork:
- ✧ 450 g pork steak, cut in cubes
- ✧ 1 tablespoon white wine vinegar
- ✧ 3 tablespoons steak sauce or brown sauce
- ✧ 60 ml soy sauce
- ✧ 1 teaspoon powdered chili
- ✧ 1 teaspoon red chilli flakes
- ✧ 2 teaspoons smoked paprika
- ✧ 1 teaspoon garlic salt
- ✧ For the Vegetable:
- ✧ 1 courgette, cut in cubes
- ✧ 1 butternut marrow, deseeded and cut in cubes
- ✧ 1 red pepper, cut in cubes
- ✧ 1 green pepper, cut in cubes
- ✧ Salt and ground black pepper, to taste
- ✧ Cooking spray
- ✧ Special Equipment:
- ✧ 4 bamboo skewers, soaked in water for at least 30 minutes

Instructions

1. Combine the ingredients for the pork in a large bowl. Press the pork to dunk in the marinade. Wrap the bowl in plastic and refrigerate for at least an hour. 2. Preheat the air fryer to 190°C and spritz with cooking spray. 3. Remove the pork from the marinade and run the skewers through the pork and vegetables alternatively. Sprinkle with salt and pepper to taste. 4. Arrange the skewers in the preheated air fryer and spritz with cooking spray. Air fry for 8 minutes or until the pork is browned and the vegetables are lightly charred and tender. Flip the skewers halfway through. You may need to work in batches to avoid overcrowding. 5. Serve immediately.

Cajun Bacon Pork Loin Fillet

Preparation time: 30 minutes | Cook time: 20 minutes | Serves 6

- ✧ 680 g pork loin fillet or pork tenderloin
- ✧ 3 tablespoons olive oil
- ✧ 2 tablespoons Cajun spice mix
- ✧ Salt, to taste
- ✧ 6 slices bacon
- ✧ Olive oil spray

Instructions

1. Cut the pork in half so that it will fit in the air fryer basket. 2. Place both pieces of meat in a resealable plastic bag. Add the oil, Cajun seasoning, and salt to taste, if using. Seal the bag and massage to coat all of the meat with the oil and seasonings. Marinate in the refrigerator for at least 1 hour or up to 24 hours. 3. Remove the pork from the bag and wrap 3 bacon slices around each piece. Spray the air fryer basket with olive oil spray. Place the meat in the air fryer. Set the air fryer to 180°C for 15 minutes. Increase the temperature to 200°C for 5 minutes. Use a meat thermometer to ensure the meat has reached an internal temperature of 64°C. 4. Let the meat rest for 10 minutes. Slice into 6

medallions and serve.

Mediterranean Beef Steaks

Preparation time: 20 minutes | Cook time: 20 minutes | Serves 4

- ✧ 2 tablespoons soy sauce or tamari
- ✧ 3 heaping tablespoons fresh chives
- ✧ 2 tablespoons olive oil
- ✧ 3 tablespoons dry white wine
- ✧ 4 small-sized beef steaks
- ✧ 2 teaspoons smoked cayenne pepper
- ✧ ½ teaspoon dried basil
- ✧ ½ teaspoon dried rosemary
- ✧ 1 teaspoon freshly ground black pepper
- ✧ 1 teaspoon sea salt, or more to taste

Instructions

1. Firstly, coat the steaks with the cayenne pepper, black pepper, salt, basil, and rosemary. 2. Drizzle the steaks with olive oil, white wine, and soy sauce. 3. Finally, roast in the air fryer for 20 minutes at 170°C. Serve garnished with fresh chives. Bon appétit!

Panko Pork Chops

Preparation time: 10 minutes | Cook time: 12 minutes | Serves 4

- ✧ 4 boneless pork chops, excess fat trimmed
- ✧ ¼ teaspoon salt
- ✧ 2 eggs
- ✧ 130 g panko bread crumbs
- ✧ 3 tablespoons grated Parmesan cheese
- ✧ 1½ teaspoons paprika
- ✧ ½ teaspoon granulated garlic
- ✧ ½ teaspoon onion granules
- ✧ 1 teaspoon chilli powder
- ✧ ¼ teaspoon freshly ground black pepper
- ✧ Olive oil spray

Instructions

1. Sprinkle the pork chops with salt on both sides and let them sit while you prepare the seasonings and egg wash. 2. In a shallow medium bowl, beat the eggs. 3. In another shallow medium bowl, stir together the

panko, Parmesan cheese, paprika, granulated garlic, onion granules, chilli powder, and pepper. 4. Dip the pork chops in the egg and in the panko mixture to coat. Firmly press the crumbs onto the chops. 5. Insert the crisper plate into the basket and the basket into the unit. Preheat the unit by selecting AIR ROAST, setting the temperature to 200°C, and setting the time to 3 minutes. Select START/STOP to begin. 6. Once the unit is preheated, spray the crisper plate with olive oil. Place the pork chops into the basket and spray them with olive oil. 7. Select AIR ROAST, set the temperature to 200°C, and set the time to 12 minutes. Select START/STOP to begin. 8. After 6 minutes, flip the pork chops and spray them with more olive oil. Resume cooking. 9. When the cooking is complete, the chops should be golden and crispy and a food thermometer should register 64°C. Serve immediately.

Crescent Dogs

Preparation time: 15 minutes | Cook time: 8 minutes | Makes 24 crescent dogs

- ✧ Oil, for spraying
- ✧ 1 (230 g) tin ready-to-bake croissants
- ✧ 8 slices Cheddar cheese, cut into thirds
- ✧ 24 cocktail bangers or 8 (6-inch) hot dogs, cut into thirds
- ✧ 2 tablespoons unsalted melted butter
- ✧ 1 tablespoon sea salt flakes

Instructions

1. Line the air fryer basket with parchment and spray lightly with oil. 2. Separate the dough into 8 triangles. Cut each triangle into 3 narrow triangles so you have 24 total triangles. 3. Top each triangle with 1 piece of cheese and 1 cocktail banger. 4. Roll up each piece of dough, starting at the wide end and rolling toward the point. 5. Place the rolls in the prepared basket in a single layer. You may need to cook in batches, depending on

the size of your air fryer. 6. Air fry at 160°C for 3 to 4 minutes, flip, and cook for another 3 to 4 minutes, or until golden brown. 7. Brush with the melted butter and sprinkle with the sea salt flakes before serving.

Chuck Kebab with Rocket

Preparation time: 30 minutes | Cook time: 25 minutes | Serves 4

- ✧ 120 g leeks, chopped
- ✧ 2 garlic cloves, smashed
- ✧ 900 g beef mince
- ✧ Salt, to taste
- ✧ ¼ teaspoon ground black pepper, or more to taste
- ✧ 1 teaspoon cayenne pepper
- ✧ ½ teaspoon ground sumac
- ✧ 3 saffron threads
- ✧ 2 tablespoons loosely packed fresh flat-leaf parsley leaves
- ✧ 4 tablespoons tahini sauce
- ✧ 110 g baby rocket
- ✧ 1 tomato, cut into slices

Instructions

1. In a bowl, mix the chopped leeks, garlic, beef mince, and spices; knead with your hands until everything is well incorporated. 2. Now, mound the beef mixture around a wooden skewer into a pointed-ended banger. 3. Cook in the preheated air fryer at 180°C for 25 minutes. Serve your kebab with the tahini sauce, baby rocket and tomato. Enjoy!

Parmesan-Crusted Pork Chops

Preparation time: 5 minutes | Cook time: 12 minutes | Serves 4

- ✧ 1 large egg
- ✧ 120 g grated Parmesan cheese
- ✧ 4 (110 g) boneless pork chops
- ✧ ½ teaspoon salt
- ✧ ¼ teaspoon ground black pepper

Instructions

1. Whisk egg in a medium bowl and place Parmesan in a separate medium bowl. 2.

Sprinkle pork chops on both sides with salt and pepper. Dip each pork chop into egg, then press both sides into Parmesan. 3. Place pork chops into ungreased air fryer basket. Adjust the temperature to 200°C and air fry for 12 minutes, turning chops halfway through cooking. Pork chops will be golden and have an internal temperature of at least 64°C when done. Serve warm.

Filipino Crispy Pork Belly

Preparation time: 20 minutes | Cook time: 30 minutes | Serves 4

✧ 450 g pork belly
✧ 700 ml water
✧ 6 garlic cloves
✧ 2 tablespoons soy sauce
✧ 1 teaspoon coarse or flaky salt
✧ 1 teaspoon black pepper
✧ 2 bay leaves

Instructions

1. Cut the pork belly into three thick chunks so it will cook more evenly. 2. Place the pork, water, garlic, soy sauce, salt, pepper, and bay leaves in the inner pot of an Instant Pot or other electric pressure cooker. Seal and cook at high pressure for 15 minutes. Let the pressure release naturally for 10 minutes, then manually release the remaining pressure. (If you do not have a pressure cooker, place all the ingredients in a large saucepan. Cover and cook over low heat until a knife tin be easily inserted into the skin side of pork belly, about 1 hour.) Using tongs, very carefully transfer the meat to a wire rack over a rimmed baking sheet to drain and dry for 10 minutes. 3. Cut each chunk of pork belly into two long slices. Arrange the slices in the air fryer basket. Set the air fryer to 200°C for 15 minutes, or until the fat has crisped. 4. Serve immediately.

Chicken-Fried Steak

Preparation time: 20 minutes | Cook time: 14 minutes | Serves 2

✧ Steak:
✧ Oil, for spraying
✧ 90 g plain flour
✧ 1 teaspoon salt
✧ 1 teaspoon freshly ground black pepper
✧ ½ teaspoon paprika
✧ ½ teaspoon onion granules
✧ 1 teaspoon granulated garlic
✧ 180 g buttermilk
✧ ½ teaspoon hot sauce
✧ 2 (140 g) minute steaks
✧ Gravy:
✧ 2 tablespoons unsalted butter
✧ 2 tablespoons plain flour
✧ 235 ml milk
✧ ½ teaspoon salt
✧ ½ teaspoon freshly ground black pepper

Make the Steak **Instructions**

1. Line the air fryer basket with parchment and spray lightly with oil. 2. In a medium bowl, mix together the flour, salt, black pepper, paprika, onion granules, and garlic. 3. In another bowl, whisk together the buttermilk and hot sauce. 4. Dredge the steaks in the flour mixture, dip in the buttermilk mixture, and dredge again in the flour until completely coated. Shake off any excess flour. 5. Place the steaks in the prepared basket and spray liberally with oil. 6. Air fry at 200°C for 7 minutes, flip, spray with oil, and cook for another 6 to 7 minutes, or until crispy and browned. Make the Gravy 7. In a small saucepan, whisk together the butter and flour over medium heat until the butter is melted. Slowly add the milk, salt, and black pepper, increase the heat to medium-high, and continue to cook, stirring constantly, until the mixture thickens. Remove from the heat. 8. Transfer the steaks to plates and pour the gravy over the top. Serve immediately.

Buttery Pork Chops

Preparation time: 5 minutes | Cook time: 12 minutes | Serves 4

✧   4 (110 g) boneless pork chops
✧   ½ teaspoon salt
✧   ¼ teaspoon ground black pepper
✧   2 tablespoons salted butter, softened

Instructions

1. Sprinkle pork chops on all sides with salt and pepper. Place chops into ungreased air fryer basket in a single layer. Adjust the temperature to 200°C and air fry for 12 minutes. Pork chops will be golden and have an internal temperature of at least 64°C when done. 2. Use tongs to remove cooked pork chops from air fryer and place onto a large plate. Top each chop with ½ tablespoon butter and let sit 2 minutes to melt. Serve warm.

Short Ribs with Chimichurri

Preparation time: 30 minutes | Cook time: 13 minutes | Serves 4

✧   450 g boneless short ribs
✧   1½ teaspoons sea salt, divided
✧   ½ teaspoon freshly ground black pepper, divided
✧   120 g fresh parsley leaves
✧   120 g fresh coriander leaves
✧   1 teaspoon minced garlic
✧   1 tablespoon freshly squeezed lemon juice
✧   ½ teaspoon ground cumin
✧   ¼ teaspoon red pepper flakes
✧   2 tablespoons extra-virgin olive oil
✧   Avocado oil spray

Instructions

1. Pat the short ribs dry with paper towels. Sprinkle the ribs all over with 1 teaspoon salt and ¼ teaspoon black pepper. Let sit at room temperature for 45 minutes. 2. Meanwhile, place the parsley, coriander, garlic, lemon juice, cumin, red pepper flakes, the remaining ½ teaspoon salt, and the remaining ¼ teaspoon black pepper in a blender or food processor. With the blender running, slowly drizzle in the olive oil. Blend for about 1 minute, until the mixture is smooth and well combined. 3. Set the air fryer to 200°C. Spray both sides of the ribs with oil. Place in the basket and air fry for 8 minutes. Flip and cook for another 5 minutes, until an instant-read thermometer reads 52°C for medium-rare (or to your desired doneness). 4. Allow the meat to rest for 5 to 10 minutes, then slice. Serve warm with the chimichurri sauce.

Pork Loin Back Ribs

Preparation time: 5 minutes | Cook time: 25 minutes | Serves 4

✧   900 g pork loin Back Ribs
✧   2 teaspoons chilli powder
✧   1 teaspoon paprika
✧   ½ teaspoon onion granules
✧   ½ teaspoon garlic powder
✧   ¼ teaspoon ground cayenne pepper
✧   120 ml low-carb, sugar-free barbecue sauce

Instructions

1. Rub ribs with all ingredients except barbecue sauce. Place into the air fryer basket. 2. Adjust the temperature to 200°C and roast for 25 minutes. 3. When done, ribs will be dark and charred with an internal temperature of at least 85°C. Brush ribs with barbecue sauce and serve warm.

Beef Burgers with Mushroom

Preparation time: 10 minutes | Cook time: 21 to 23 minutes | Serves 4

✧   450 g beef mince, formed into 4 patties
✧   Sea salt and freshly ground black pepper, to taste
✧   235 g thinly sliced onion
✧   230 g mushrooms, sliced
✧   1 tablespoon avocado oil

- ✧ 60 g Gruyère cheese, shredded (about 120 ml)

Instructions

1. Season the patties on both sides with salt and pepper. 2. Set the air fryer to 190°C. Place the patties in the basket and cook for 3 minutes. Flip and cook for another 2 minutes. Remove the burgers and set aside. 3. Place the onion and mushrooms in a medium bowl. Add the avocado oil and salt and pepper to taste; toss well. 4. Place the onion and mushrooms in the air fryer basket. Cook for 15 minutes, stirring occasionally. 5. Spoon the onions and mushrooms over the patties. Top with the cheese. Place the patties back in the air fryer basket and cook for another 1 to 3 minutes, until the cheese melts and an instant-read thermometer reads 72°C. Remove and let rest. The temperature will rise to 74°C, yielding a perfect medium-well burger.

Mojito Lamb Chops

Preparation time: 30 minutes | Cook time: 5 minutes | Serves 2

- ✧ Marinade:
- ✧ 2 teaspoons grated lime zest
- ✧ 120 ml lime juice
- ✧ 60 ml avocado oil
- ✧ 60 g chopped fresh mint leaves
- ✧ 4 cloves garlic, roughly chopped
- ✧ 2 teaspoons fine sea salt
- ✧ ½ teaspoon ground black pepper
- ✧ 4 (1-inch-thick) lamb chops
- ✧ Sprigs of fresh mint, for garnish (optional)
- ✧ Lime slices, for serving (optional)

Instructions

1. Make the marinade: Place all the ingredients for the marinade in a food processor or blender and purée until mostly smooth with a few small chunks. Transfer half of the marinade to a shallow dish and set the other half aside for serving. Add the lamb to the shallow dish, cover, and place in the refrigerator to marinate for at least 2 hours or overnight. 2. Spray the air fryer basket with avocado oil. Preheat the air fryer to 200°C. 3. Remove the chops from the marinade and place them in the air fryer basket. Air fry for 5 minutes, or until the internal temperature reaches 64°C for medium doneness. 4. Allow the chops to rest for 10 minutes before serving with the rest of the marinade as a sauce. Garnish with fresh mint leaves and serve with lime slices, if desired. Best served fresh.

Orange-Mustard Glazed Salmon

Preparation time: 10 minutes | Cook time: 10 minutes | Serves 2

- ✧ 1 tablespoon orange marmalade
- ✧ ¼ teaspoon grated orange zest plus 1 tablespoon juice
- ✧ 2 teaspoons whole-grain mustard
- ✧ 2 (230 g) skin-on salmon fillets, 1½ inches thick
- ✧ Salt and pepper, to taste
- ✧ Vegetable oil spray

Instructions

1. Preheat the air fryer to 200ºC. 2. Make foil sling for air fryer basket by folding 1 long sheet of aluminium foil so it is 4 inches wide. Lay sheet of foil widthwise across basket, pressing foil into and up sides of basket. Fold excess foil as needed so that edges of foil are flush with top of basket. Lightly spray foil and basket with vegetable oil spray. 3. Combine marmalade, orange zest and juice, and mustard in bowl. Pat salmon dry with paper towels and season with salt and pepper. Brush tops and sides of fillets evenly with glaze. Arrange fillets skin side down on sling in prepared basket, spaced evenly apart. Air fry salmon until center is still translucent when checked with the tip of a paring knife and registers 52ºC (for medium-rare), 10 to 14 minutes, using sling to rotate fillets halfway through cooking. 4. Using the sling, carefully remove salmon from air fryer. Slide fish spatula along underside of fillets and transfer to individual serving plates, leaving skin behind. Serve.

Lemon Pepper Prawns

Preparation time: 15 minutes | Cook time: 8 minutes | Serves 2

- ✧ Olive or vegetable oil, for spraying
- ✧ 340 g medium raw prawns, peeled and deveined
- ✧ 3 tablespoons lemon juice
- ✧ 1 tablespoon olive oil
- ✧ 1 teaspoon lemon pepper
- ✧ ¼ teaspoon paprika
- ✧ ¼ teaspoon granulated garlic

Instructions

1. Preheat the air fryer to 200ºC. Line the air fryer basket with baking paper and spray lightly with oil. 2. In a medium bowl, toss together the prawns, lemon juice, olive oil, lemon pepper, paprika, and garlic until evenly coated. 3. Place the prawns in the prepared basket. 4. Cook for 6 to 8 minutes, or until pink and firm. Serve immediately.

Crab Cakes with Sriracha Mayonnaise

Preparation time: 15 minutes | Cook time: 10 minutes | Serves 4

- ✧ Sriracha Mayonnaise:
- ✧ 230 g mayonnaise
- ✧ 1 tablespoon Sriracha
- ✧ 1½ teaspoons freshly squeezed lemon juice
- ✧ Crab Cakes:
- ✧ 1 teaspoon extra-virgin olive oil
- ✧ 40 g finely diced red pepper
- ✧ 40 g diced onion
- ✧ 40 g diced celery
- ✧ 455 g lump crab meat
- ✧ 1 teaspoon Old Bay seasoning
- ✧ 1 egg
- ✧ 1½ teaspoons freshly squeezed lemon juice
- ✧ 100 g panko bread crumbs, divided
- ✧ Vegetable oil, for spraying

Instructions

1. Mix the mayonnaise, Sriracha, and lemon juice in a small bowl. Place ⅔ of the mixture in a separate bowl to form the base of the crab cakes. Cover the remaining Sriracha mayonnaise and refrigerate. (This will become dipping sauce for the crab cakes once they are cooked.) 2. Heat the olive oil in a heavy-bottomed, medium frying pan over medium-high heat. Add the pepper, onion, and celery and sauté for 3 minutes. Transfer the vegetables to the bowl with the reserved ⅔ of Sriracha mayonnaise. Mix in the crab, Old Bay seasoning, egg, and lemon juice. Add 120 g of the panko. Form the crab mixture into 8 cakes. Dredge the cakes in the remaining panko, turning to coat. Place on a baking sheet. Cover and refrigerate for at least 1 hour and up to 8 hours. 3. Preheat the air fryer to 190°C. Spray the air fryer basket with oil. Working in batches as needed so as not to overcrowd the basket, place the chilled crab cakes in a single layer in the basket. Spray the crab cakes with oil. Bake until golden brown, 8 to 10 minutes, carefully turning halfway through cooking. Remove to a platter and keep warm. Repeat with the remaining crab cakes as needed. Serve the crab cakes immediately with Sriracha mayonnaise dipping sauce.

Trout Amandine with Lemon Butter Sauce

Preparation time: 20 minutes | Cook time: 8 minutes | Serves 4

Trout Amandine:

65 g toasted almonds

30 g grated Parmesan cheese

1 teaspoon salt

½ teaspoon freshly ground black pepper

2 tablespoons butter, melted

4 trout fillets, or salmon fillets, 110 g each

Cooking spray

Lemon Butter Sauce:

8 tablespoons butter, melted

2 tablespoons freshly squeezed lemon juice

½ teaspoon Worcestershire sauce

½ teaspoon salt

½ teaspoon freshly ground black pepper

¼ teaspoon hot sauce

Instructions

1. In a blender or food processor, pulse the almonds for 5 to 10 seconds until finely processed. Transfer to a shallow bowl and whisk in the Parmesan cheese, salt, and pepper. Place the melted butter in another shallow bowl. 2. One at a time, dip the fish in the melted butter, then the almond mixture, coating thoroughly. 3. Preheat the air fryer to 150°C. Line the air fryer basket with baking paper. 4. Place the coated fish on the baking paper and spritz with oil. 5. Bake for 4 minutes. Flip the fish, spritz it with oil, and bake for 4 minutes more until the fish flakes easily with a fork. 6. In a small bowl, whisk the butter, lemon juice, Worcestershire sauce, salt, pepper, and hot sauce until blended. 7. Serve with the fish.

Friday Night Fish-Fry

Preparation time: 10 minutes | Cook time: 10 minutes | Serves 4

- ✧ 1 large egg
- ✧ 25 g powdered Parmesan cheese
- ✧ 1 teaspoon smoked paprika
- ✧ ¼ teaspoon celery salt
- ✧ ¼ teaspoon ground black pepper
- ✧ 4 cod fillets, 110 g each
- ✧ Chopped fresh oregano or parsley, for garnish (optional)
- ✧ Lemon slices, for serving (optional)

Instructions

1. Spray the air fryer basket with avocado oil.

Preheat the air fryer to 200ºC. 2. Crack the egg in a shallow bowl and beat it lightly with a fork. Combine the Parmesan cheese, paprika, celery salt, and pepper in a separate shallow bowl. 3. One at a time, dip the fillets into the egg, then dredge them in the Parmesan mixture. Using your hands, press the Parmesan onto the fillets to form a nice crust. As you finish, place the fish in the air fryer basket. 4. Air fry the fish in the air fryer for 10 minutes, or until it is cooked through and flakes easily with a fork. Garnish with fresh oregano or parsley and serve with lemon slices, if desired. 5. Store leftovers in an airtight container in the refrigerator for up to 3 days. Reheat in a preheated 200ºC air fryer for 5 minutes, or until warmed through.

Tuna Patties with Spicy Sriracha Sauce

Preparation time: 10 minutes | Cook time: 10 minutes | Serves 4

- ✧ 2 (170 g) cans tuna packed in oil, drained
- ✧ 3 tablespoons almond flour
- ✧ 2 tablespoons mayonnaise
- ✧ 1 teaspoon dried dill
- ✧ ½ teaspoon onion powder
- ✧ Pinch of salt and pepper
- ✧ Spicy Sriracha Sauce:
- ✧ 60 g mayonnaise
- ✧ 1 tablespoon Sriracha sauce
- ✧ 1 teaspoon garlic powder

Instructions

1. Preheat the air fryer to 190ºC. Line the basket with baking paper. 2. In a large bowl, combine the tuna, almond flour, mayonnaise, dill, and onion powder. Season to taste with salt and freshly ground black pepper. Use a fork to stir, mashing with the back of the fork as necessary, until thoroughly combined. 3. Use an ice cream scoop to form the tuna mixture patties. Place the patties in a single layer on the baking paper in the air fryer basket. Press lightly with the bottom of the scoop to flatten into a circle about ½ inch thick. Pausing halfway through the cooking time to turn the patties, air fry for 10 minutes until lightly browned. 4. To make the Sriracha sauce: In a small bowl, combine the mayonnaise, Sriracha, and garlic powder. Serve the tuna patties topped with the Sriracha sauce.

Salmon Spring Rolls

Preparation time: 20 minutes | Cook time: 8 to 10 minutes | Serves 4

- ✧ 230 g salmon fillet
- ✧ 1 teaspoon toasted sesame oil
- ✧ 1 onion, sliced
- ✧ 8 rice paper wrappers
- ✧ 1 yellow pepper, thinly sliced
- ✧ 1 carrot, shredded
- ✧ 10 g chopped fresh flat-leaf parsley
- ✧ 15 g chopped fresh basil

Instructions

1. Put the salmon in the air fryer basket and drizzle with the sesame oil. Add the onion. Air fry at 190ºC for 8 to 10 minutes, or until the salmon just flakes when tested with a fork and the onion is tender. 2. Meanwhile, fill a small shallow bowl with warm water. One at a time, dip the rice paper wrappers into the water and place on a work surface. 3. Top each wrapper with one-eighth each of the salmon and onion mixture, yellow pepper, carrot, parsley, and basil. Roll up the wrapper, folding in the sides, to enclose the ingredients. 4. If you like, bake in the air fryer at 190ºC for 7 to 9 minutes, until the rolls are crunchy. Cut the rolls in half to serve.

Greek Fish Pitas

Preparation time: 10 minutes | Cook time: 15 minutes | Serves 4

- ✧ 455 g pollock, cut into 1-inch pieces

- 60 ml olive oil
- 1 teaspoon salt
- ½ teaspoon dried oregano
- ½ teaspoon dried thyme
- ½ teaspoon garlic powder
- ¼ teaspoon cayenne
- 4 whole wheat pitas
- 75 g shredded lettuce
- 2 plum tomatoes, diced
- Nonfat plain Greek yoghurt
- Lemon, quartered

Instructions

1. Preheat the air fryer to 190°C. 2. In a medium bowl, combine the pollock with olive oil, salt, oregano, thyme, garlic powder, and cayenne. 3. Put the pollock into the air fryer basket and roast for 15 minutes. 4. Serve inside pitas with lettuce, tomato, and Greek yoghurt with a lemon wedge on the side.

Prawns Curry

Preparation time: 30 minutes | Cook time: 10 minutes | Serves 4

- 180 ml unsweetened full-fat coconut milk
- 10 g finely chopped brown onion
- 2 teaspoons garam masala
- 1 tablespoon minced fresh ginger
- 1 tablespoon minced garlic
- 1 teaspoon ground turmeric
- 1 teaspoon salt
- ¼ to ½ teaspoon cayenne pepper
- 455 g raw prawns (21 to 25 count), peeled and deveined
- 2 teaspoons chopped fresh coriander

Instructions

1. In a large bowl, stir together the coconut milk, onion, garam masala, ginger, garlic, turmeric, salt and cayenne, until well blended. 2. Add the prawns and toss until coated with sauce on all sides. Marinate at room temperature for 30 minutes. 3. Transfer the prawns and marinade to a baking pan. Place the pan in the air fryer basket. Set the air fryer to 190°C for 10 minutes, stirring halfway through the cooking time. 4. Transfer the prawns to a serving bowl or platter. Sprinkle with the coriander and serve.

Prawns with Swiss Chard

Preparation time: 10 minutes | Cook time: 10 minutes | Serves 4

- 455 g prawns, peeled and deveined
- ½ teaspoon smoked paprika
- 70 g Swiss chard, chopped
- 2 tablespoons apple cider vinegar
- 1 tablespoon coconut oil
- 60 ml double cream

Instructions

1. Mix prawns with smoked paprika and apple cider vinegar. 2. Put the prawns in the air fryer and add coconut oil. 3. Cook the prawns at 180°C for 10 minutes. 4. Then mix cooked prawns with remaining ingredients and carefully mix.

Cornmeal-Crusted Trout Fingers

Preparation time: 15 minutes | Cook time: 6 minutes | Serves 2

- 70 g yellow cornmeal, medium or finely ground (not coarse)
- 20 g plain flour
- 1½ teaspoons baking powder
- 1 teaspoon kosher or coarse sea salt, plus more as needed
- ½ teaspoon freshly ground black pepper, plus more as needed
- ⅛ teaspoon cayenne pepper
- 340 g skinless trout fillets, cut into strips 1 inch wide and 3 inches long
- 3 large eggs, lightly beaten
- Cooking spray
- 115 g mayonnaise
- 2 tablespoons capers, rinsed and finely chopped
- 1 tablespoon fresh tarragon
- 1 teaspoon fresh lemon juice, plus lemon

wedges, for serving

Instructions

1. Preheat the air fryer to 200ºC. 2. In a large bowl, whisk together the cornmeal, flour, baking powder, salt, black pepper, and cayenne. Dip the trout strips in the egg, then toss them in the cornmeal mixture until fully coated. Transfer the trout to a rack set over a baking sheet and liberally spray all over with cooking spray. 3. Transfer half the fish to the air fryer and air fry until the fish is cooked through and golden brown, about 6 minutes. Transfer the fish fingers to a plate and repeat with the remaining fish. 4. Meanwhile, in a bowl, whisk together the mayonnaise, capers, tarragon, and lemon juice. Season the tartar sauce with salt and black pepper. 5. Serve the trout fingers hot along with the tartar sauce and lemon wedges.

Tuna-Stuffed Tomatoes

Preparation time: 5 minutes | Cook time: 5 minutes | Serves 2

- ✧ 2 medium beefsteak tomatoes, tops removed, seeded, membranes removed
- ✧ 2 (75 g) g tuna fillets packed in water, drained
- ✧ 1 medium stalk celery, trimmed and chopped
- ✧ 2 tablespoons mayonnaise
- ✧ ¼ teaspoon salt
- ✧ ¼ teaspoon ground black pepper
- ✧ 2 teaspoons coconut oil
- ✧ 25 g shredded mild Cheddar cheese

Instructions

1. Scoop pulp out of each tomato, leaving ½-inch shell. 2. In a medium bowl, mix tuna, celery, mayonnaise, salt, and pepper. Drizzle with coconut oil. Spoon ½ mixture into each tomato and top each with 2 tablespoons Cheddar. 3. Place tomatoes into ungreased air fryer basket. Adjust the temperature to 160ºC and air fry for 5 minutes. Cheese will be melted when done. Serve warm.

Marinated Salmon Fillets

Preparation time: 10 minutes | Cook time: 15 to 20 minutes | Serves 4

- ✧ 60 ml soy sauce
- ✧ 60 ml rice wine vinegar
- ✧ 1 tablespoon brown sugar
- ✧ 1 tablespoon olive oil
- ✧ 1 teaspoon mustard powder
- ✧ 1 teaspoon ground ginger
- ✧ ½ teaspoon freshly ground black pepper
- ✧ ½ teaspoon minced garlic
- ✧ 4 salmon fillets, 170 g each, skin-on
- ✧ Cooking spray

Instructions

1. In a small bowl, combine the soy sauce, rice wine vinegar, brown sugar, olive oil, mustard powder, ginger, black pepper, and garlic to make a marinade. 2. Place the fillets in a shallow baking dish and pour the marinade over them. Cover the baking dish and marinate for at least 1 hour in the refrigerator, turning the fillets occasionally to keep them coated in the marinade. 3. Preheat the air fryer to 190ºC. Spray the air fryer basket lightly with cooking spray. 4. Shake off as much marinade as possible from the fillets and place them, skin-side down, in the air fryer basket in a single layer. You may need to cook the fillets in batches. 5. Air fry for 15 to 20 minutes for well done. The minimum internal temperature should be 64ºC at the thickest part of the fillets. 6. Serve hot.

Lemony Salmon

Preparation time: 30 minutes | Cook time: 10 minutes | Serves 4

- ✧ 680 g salmon steak
- ✧ ½ teaspoon grated lemon zest
- ✧ Freshly cracked mixed peppercorns, to taste
- ✧ 80 ml lemon juice
- ✧ Fresh chopped chives, for garnish

- 120 ml dry white wine, or apple cider vinegar
- ½ teaspoon fresh coriander, chopped
- Fine sea salt, to taste

Instructions

1. To prepare the marinade, place all ingredients, except for salmon steak and chives, in a deep pan. Bring to a boil over medium-high flame until it has reduced by half. Allow it to cool down. 2. After that, allow salmon steak to marinate in the refrigerator approximately 40 minutes. Discard the marinade and transfer the fish steak to the preheated air fryer. 3. Air fry at 200°C for 9 to 10 minutes. To finish, brush hot fish steaks with the reserved marinade, garnish with fresh chopped chives, and serve right away!

Tilapia Almondine

Preparation time: 10 minutes | Cook time: 10 minutes | Serves 2

- 25 g almond flour or fine dried bread crumbs
- 2 tablespoons salted butter or ghee, melted
- 1 teaspoon black pepper
- ½ teaspoon kosher or coarse sea salt
- 60 g mayonnaise
- 2 tilapia fillets
- 435 g thinly sliced almonds
- Vegetable oil spray

Instructions

1. In a small bowl, mix together the almond flour, butter, pepper and salt. 2. Spread the mayonnaise on both sides of each fish fillet. Dredge the fillets in the almond flour mixture. Spread the sliced almonds on one side of each fillet, pressing lightly to adhere. 3. Spray the air fryer basket with vegetable oil spray. Place the fish fillets in the basket. Set the air fryer to 160°C for 10 minutes, or until the fish flakes easily with a fork.

Lemon Mahi-Mahi

Preparation time: 5 minutes | Cook time: 14 minutes | Serves 2

- Olive or vegetable oil, for spraying
- 2 (170 g) dolphinfish
- 1 tablespoon lemon juice
- 1 tablespoon olive oil
- ¼ teaspoon salt
- ¼ teaspoon freshly ground black pepper
- 1 tablespoon chopped fresh dill
- 2 lemon slices

Instructions

1. Line the air fryer basket with baking paper and spray lightly with oil. 2. Place the mahi-mahi in the prepared basket. 3. In a small bowl, whisk together the lemon juice and olive oil. Brush the mixture evenly over the mahi-mahi. 4. Sprinkle the mahi-mahi with the salt and black pepper and top with the dill. 5. Air fry at 200°C for 12 to 14 minutes, depending on the thickness of the fillets, until they flake easily. 6. Transfer to plates, top each with a lemon slice, and serve.

Mackerel with Spinach

Preparation time: 15 minutes | Cook time: 20 minutes | Serves 5

- 455 g mackerel, trimmed
- 1 pepper, chopped
- 15 g spinach, chopped
- 1 tablespoon avocado oil
- 1 teaspoon ground black pepper
- 1 teaspoon tomato paste

Instructions

1. In the mixing bowl, mix pepper with spinach, ground black pepper, and tomato paste. 2. Fill the mackerel with spinach mixture. 3. Then brush the fish with avocado oil and put it in the air fryer. 4. Cook the fish at 190°C for 20 minutes.

Sweet Tilapia Fillets

Preparation time: 5 minutes | Cook time: 14 minutes | Serves 4

- ✧ 2 tablespoons granulated sweetener
- ✧ 1 tablespoon apple cider vinegar
- ✧ 4 tilapia fillets, boneless
- ✧ 1 teaspoon olive oil

Instructions

1. Mix apple cider vinegar with olive oil and sweetener. 2. Then rub the tilapia fillets with the sweet mixture and put in the air fryer basket in one layer. Cook the fish at 180°C for 7 minutes per side.

Tilapia with Pecans

Preparation time: 20 minutes | Cook time: 16 minutes | Serves 5

- ✧ 2 tablespoons ground flaxseeds
- ✧ 1 teaspoon paprika
- ✧ Sea salt and white pepper, to taste
- ✧ 1 teaspoon garlic paste
- ✧ 2 tablespoons extra-virgin olive oil
- ✧ 65 g pecans, ground
- ✧ 5 tilapia fillets, sliced into halves

Instructions

1. Combine the ground flaxseeds, paprika, salt, white pepper, garlic paste, olive oil, and ground pecans in a sealable freezer bag. Add the fish fillets and shake to coat well. 2. Spritz the air fryer basket with cooking spray. Cook in the preheated air fryer at 200°C for 10 minutes; turn them over and cook for 6 minutes more. Work in batches. 3. Serve with lemon wedges, if desired. Enjoy!

Teriyaki Shrimp Skewers

Preparation time: 10 minutes | Cook time: 6 minutes | Makes 12 skewered shrimp

- ✧ 1½ tablespoons mirin
- ✧ 1½ teaspoons ginger paste
- ✧ 1½ tablespoons soy sauce
- ✧ 12 large shrimp, peeled and deveined
- ✧ 1 large egg
- ✧ 90 g panko breadcrumbs
- ✧ Cooking spray

Instructions

1. Combine the mirin, ginger paste, and soy sauce in a large bowl 2.Stir to mix well 3.Dunk the shrimp in the bowl of mirin mixture, then wrap the bowl in plastic and refrigerate for 1 hour to marinate 4.Preheat the air fryer to 200°C 5.Spritz the air fryer basket with cooking spray 6.Run twelve 4-inch skewers through each shrimp 7.Whisk the egg in the bowl of marinade to combine well 8.Pour the breadcrumbs on a plate 9.Dredge the shrimp skewers in the egg mixture, then shake the excess off and roll over the breadcrumbs to coat well 10.Arrange the shrimp skewers in the preheated air fryer and spritz with cooking spray 1Instructions 1.You need to work in batches to avoid overcrowding 12.Air fry for 6 minutes or until the shrimp are opaque and firm 13.Flip the shrimp skewers halfway through 14.Serve immediately.

Popcorn Prawns

Preparation time: 15 minutes | Cook time: 18 to 20 minutes | Serves 4

- ✧ 35 g plain flour, plus 2 tablespoons
- ✧ ½ teaspoon garlic powder
- ✧ 1½ teaspoons Old Bay Seasoning
- ✧ ½ teaspoon onion powder
- ✧ 120 ml beer, plus 2 tablespoons
- ✧ 340 g prawns, peeled and deveined
- ✧ Olive oil for misting or cooking spray
- ✧ Coating:
- ✧ 180 g panko crumbs
- ✧ 1 teaspoon Old Bay Seasoning
- ✧ ½ teaspoon ground black pepper

Instructions

1. In a large bowl, mix together the flour, garlic powder, Old Bay Seasoning, and onion powder. Stir in beer to blend. 2. Add prawns to batter and stir to coat. 3. Combine the coating ingredients in food processor and pulse to finely crush the crumbs. Transfer crumbs to shallow dish. 4. Preheat the air fryer to 200°C. 5. Pour the prawns and batter

into a colander to drain. Stir with a spoon to drain excess batter. 6. Working with a handful of prawns at a time, roll in crumbs and place on a baking sheet. 7. Spray breaded prawns with oil or cooking spray and place all at once into air fryer basket. 8. Air fry for 5 minutes. Shake basket or stir and mist again with olive oil or spray. Cook 5 more minutes, shake basket again, and mist lightly again. Continue cooking 3 to 5 more minutes, until browned and crispy.

Savoury Prawns

Preparation time: 5 minutes | Cook time: 8 to 10 minutes | Serves 4

- ✧ 455 g fresh large prawns, peeled and deveined
- ✧ 1 tablespoon avocado oil
- ✧ 2 teaspoons minced garlic, divided
- ✧ ½ teaspoon red pepper flakes
- ✧ Sea salt and freshly ground black pepper, to taste
- ✧ 2 tablespoons unsalted butter, melted
- ✧ 2 tablespoons chopped fresh parsley

Instructions

1. Place the prawns in a large bowl and toss with the avocado oil, 1 teaspoon of minced garlic, and red pepper flakes. Season with salt and pepper. 2. Set the air fryer to 180°C. Arrange the prawns in a single layer in the air fryer basket, working in batches if necessary. Cook for 6 minutes. Flip the prawns and cook for 2 to 4 minutes more, until the internal temperature of the prawns reaches 50°C. (The time it takes to cook will depend on the size of the prawns.) 3. While the prawns are cooking, melt the butter in a small saucepan over medium heat and stir in the remaining 1 teaspoon of garlic. 4. Transfer the cooked prawns to a large bowl, add the garlic butter, and toss well. Top with the parsley and serve warm.

Fish Sandwich with Tartar Sauce

Preparation time: 10 minutes | Cook time: 17 minutes | Serves 2

- ✧ Tartar Sauce:
- ✧ 115 g mayonnaise
- ✧ 2 tablespoons onion granules
- ✧ 1 dill gherkin spear, finely chopped
- ✧ 2 teaspoons gherkin juice
- ✧ ¼ teaspoon salt
- ✧ ⅛ teaspoon ground black pepper
- ✧ Fish:
- ✧ 2 tablespoons plain flour
- ✧ 1 egg, lightly beaten
- ✧ 120 g panko
- ✧ 2 teaspoons lemon pepper
- ✧ 2 tilapia fillets
- ✧ Cooking spray
- ✧ 2 soft sub rolls

Instructions

1. Preheat the air fryer to 200°C. 2. In a small bowl, combine the mayonnaise, onion granules, pickle, gherkin juice, salt, and pepper. 3. Whisk to combine and chill in the refrigerator while you make the fish. 4. Place a baking paper liner in the air fryer basket. 5. Scoop the flour out onto a plate; set aside. 6. Put the beaten egg in a medium shallow bowl. 7. On another plate, mix to combine the panko and lemon pepper. 8. Dredge the tilapia fillets in the flour, then dip in the egg, and then press into the panko mixture. 9. Place the prepared fillets on the liner in the air fryer in a single layer. 10. Spray lightly with cooking spray and air fry for 8 minutes. Carefully flip the fillets, spray with more cooking spray, and air fry for an additional 9 minutes, until golden and crispy. 1Instructions

1. Place each cooked fillet in a sub roll, top with a little bit of tartar sauce, and serve.

Crunchy Air Fried Cod Fillets

Preparation time: 10 minutes | Cook

time: 12 minutes | Serves 2

✧ 20 g panko bread crumbs
✧ 1 teaspoon vegetable oil
✧ 1 small shallot, minced
✧ 1 small garlic clove, minced
✧ ½ teaspoon minced fresh thyme
✧ Salt and pepper, to taste
✧ 1 tablespoon minced fresh parsley
✧ 1 tablespoon mayonnaise
✧ 1 large egg yolk
✧ ¼ teaspoon grated lemon zest, plus lemon wedges for serving
✧ 2 (230 g) skinless cod fillets, 1¼ inches thick
✧ Vegetable oil spray

Instructions

1. Preheat the air fryer to 150°C. 2. Make foil sling for air fryer basket by folding 1 long sheet of aluminium foil so it is 4 inches wide. Lay sheet of foil widthwise across basket, pressing foil into and up sides of basket. Fold excess foil as needed so that edges of foil are flush with top of basket. Lightly spray the foil and basket with vegetable oil spray. 3. Toss the panko with the oil in a bowl until evenly coated. Stir in the shallot, garlic, thyme, ¼ teaspoon salt, and ⅛ teaspoon pepper. Microwave, stirring frequently, until the panko is light golden brown, about 2 minutes. Transfer to a shallow dish and let cool slightly; stir in the parsley. Whisk the mayonnaise, egg yolk, lemon zest, and ⅛ teaspoon pepper together in another bowl. 4. Pat the cod dry with paper towels and season with salt and pepper. Arrange the fillets, skinned-side down, on plate and brush tops evenly with mayonnaise mixture. (Tuck thinner tail ends of fillets under themselves as needed to create uniform pieces.) Working with 1 fillet at a time, dredge the coated side in panko mixture, pressing gently to adhere. Arrange the fillets, crumb-side up, on sling in the prepared basket, spaced evenly apart. 5.

Bake for 12 to 16 minutes, using a sling to rotate fillets halfway through cooking. Using a sling, carefully remove cod from air fryer. Serve with the lemon wedges.

Sole Fillets

Preparation time: 10 minutes | Cook time: 5 to 8 minutes | Serves 4

✧ 1 egg white
✧ 1 tablespoon water
✧ 30 g panko breadcrumbs
✧ 2 tablespoons extra-light virgin olive oil
✧ 4 sole fillets, 110 g each
✧ Salt and pepper, to taste
✧ Olive or vegetable oil for misting or cooking spray

Instructions

1. Preheat the air fryer to 390°F (200°C). 2. Beat together egg white and water in shallow dish. 3. In another shallow dish, mix panko crumbs and oil until well combined and crumbly (best done by hand). 4. Season sole fillets with salt and pepper to taste. Dip each fillet into egg mixture and then roll in panko crumbs, pressing in crumbs so that fish is nicely coated. 5. Spray the air fryer basket with nonstick cooking spray and add fillets. Air fry at 200°C for 3 minutes. 6. Spray fish fillets but do not turn. Cook 2 to 5 minutes longer or until golden brown and crispy. Using a spatula, carefully remove fish from basket and serve.

Fish Cakes

Preparation time: 30 minutes | Cook time: 10 to 12 minutes | Serves 4

✧ 1 large russet potato, mashed
✧ 340 g cod or other white fish
✧ Salt and pepper, to taste
✧ Olive or vegetable oil for misting or cooking spray
✧ 1 large egg
✧ 50 g potato starch
✧ 30 g panko breadcrumbs

- ✧ 1 tablespoon fresh chopped chives
- ✧ 2 tablespoons minced onion

Instructions

1. Peel potatoes, cut into cubes, and cook on stovetop till soft. 2. Salt and pepper raw fish to taste. Mist with oil or cooking spray, and air fry at 180°C for 6 to 8 minutes, until fish flakes easily. If fish is crowded, rearrange halfway through cooking to ensure all pieces cook evenly. 3. Transfer fish to a plate and break apart to cool. 4. Beat egg in a shallow dish. 5. Place potato starch in another shallow dish, and panko crumbs in a third dish. 6. When potatoes are done, drain in colander and rinse with cold water. 7. In a large bowl, mash the potatoes and stir in the chives and onion. Add salt and pepper to taste, then stir in the fish. 8. If needed, stir in a tablespoon of the beaten egg to help bind the mixture. 9. Shape into 8 small, fat patties. Dust lightly with potato starch, dip in egg, and roll in panko crumbs. Spray both sides with oil or cooking spray. 10. Air fry for 10 to 12 minutes, until golden brown and crispy.

Air Fried Pot Stickers

Preparation time: 10 minutes | Cook time: 18 to 20 minutes | Makes 30 pot stickers

- ✧ 35 g finely chopped cabbage
- ✧ 30 g finely chopped red pepper
- ✧ 2 spring onions, finely chopped
- ✧ 1 egg, beaten
- ✧ 2 tablespoons cocktail sauce
- ✧ 2 teaspoons low-salt soy sauce
- ✧ 30 wonton wrappers
- ✧ 1 tablespoon water, for brushing the wrappers

Instructions

1. Preheat the air fryer to 180°C. 2. In a small bowl, combine the cabbage, pepper, spring onions, egg, cocktail sauce, and soy sauce, and mix well. 3. Put about 1 teaspoon of the mixture in the centre of each wonton wrapper. Fold the wrapper in half, covering the filling; dampen the edges with water, and seal. You tin crimp the edges of the wrapper with your fingers, so they look like the pot stickers you get in restaurants. Brush them with water. 4. Place the pot stickers in the air fryer basket and air fry in 2 batches for 9 to 10 minutes, or until the pot stickers are hot and the bottoms are lightly browned. 5. Serve hot.

Rumaki

Preparation time: 30 minutes | Cook time: 10 to 12 minutes per batch | Makes about 24 rumaki

- ✧ 283 g raw chicken livers
- ✧ 1 tin sliced water chestnuts, drained
- ✧ 60 ml low-salt teriyaki sauce
- ✧ 12 slices turkey bacon

Instructions

1. Cut livers into 1½-inch pieces, trimming out tough veins as you slice. 2. Place livers, water chestnuts, and teriyaki sauce in small container with lid. If needed, add another tablespoon of teriyaki sauce to make sure livers are covered. Refrigerate for 1 hour. 3. When ready to cook, cut bacon slices in half crosswise. 4. Wrap 1 piece of liver and 1 slice of water chestnut in each bacon strip. Secure with a cocktail stick. 5. When you have wrapped half of the livers, place them in the air fryer basket in a single layer. 6. Air fry at 200°C for 10 to 12 minutes, until liver is done, and bacon is crispy. 7. While first batch cooks, wrap the remaining livers. Repeat step 6 to cook your second batch.

Lemony Pear Chips

Preparation time: 15 minutes | Cook time: 9 to 13 minutes | Serves 4

- ✧ 2 firm Bosc or Anjou pears, cut crosswise into ⅛-inch-thick slices
- ✧ 1 tablespoon freshly squeezed lemon juice
- ✧ ½ teaspoon cinnamon powder
- ✧ ⅛ teaspoon ground cardamom

Instructions

1. Preheat the air fryer to 190°C. 2. Separate the smaller stem-end pear rounds from the larger rounds with seeds. Remove the core and seeds from the larger slices. Sprinkle all slices with lemon juice, cinnamon, and cardamom. 3. Put the smaller crisps into the air fryer basket. Air fry for 3 to 5 minutes, or until light golden, shaking the basket once during cooking. Remove from the air fryer. 4. Repeat with the larger slices, air frying for 6 to 8 minutes, or until light golden, shaking the basket once during cooking. 5. Remove the crisps from the air fryer. Cool and serve

or store in an airtight container at room temperature up for to 2 days.

Roasted Pearl Onion Dip

Preparation time: 5 minutes | Cook time: 12 minutes | Serves 4

- 275 g peeled pearl onions
- 3 garlic cloves
- 3 tablespoons olive oil, divided
- ½ teaspoon salt
- 240 ml non-fat plain Greek yoghurt
- 1 tablespoon lemon juice
- ¼ teaspoon black pepper
- ⅛ teaspoon red pepper flakes
- Pitta chips, mixed vegetables, or toasted bread for serving (optional)

Instructions

1. Preheat the air fryer to 180°C. 2. In a large bowl, combine the pearl onions and garlic with 2 tablespoons of the olive oil until the onions are well coated. 3. Pour the garlic-and-onion mixture into the air fryer basket and roast for 12 minutes. 4. Transfer the garlic and onions to a food processor. Pulse the mixed vegetables several times, until the onions are minced but still have some chunks. 5. In a large bowl, combine the garlic and onions and the remaining 1 tablespoon of olive oil, along with the salt, yoghurt, lemon juice, black pepper, and red pepper flakes. 6. Cover and chill for 1 hour before serving with pitta chips, mixed vegetables, or toasted bread.

Beef and Mango Skewers

Preparation time: 10 minutes | Cook time: 4 to 7 minutes | Serves 4

- 340 g beef sirloin tip, cut into 1-inch cubes
- 2 tablespoons balsamic vinegar
- 1 tablespoon olive oil
- 1 tablespoon honey
- ½ teaspoon dried marjoram
- Pinch of salt
- Freshly ground black pepper, to taste
- 1 mango

Instructions

1. Preheat the air fryer to 200°C. 2. Put the beef cubes in a medium-sized bowl and add the balsamic vinegar, olive oil, honey, marjoram, salt, and pepper. Mix well, then massage the marinade into the beef with your hands. Set aside. 3. To prepare the mango, stand it on end and cut the skin off, using a sharp knife. Then carefully cut around the oval pit to remove the flesh. Cut the mango into 1-inch cubes. 4. Thread metal skewers alternating with three beef cubes and two mango cubes. 5. Roast the skewers in the air fryer basket for 4 to 7 minutes, or until the beef is browned and at least 63°C. 6. Serve hot.

Fried Dill Pickles with Buttermilk Dressing

Preparation time: 45 minutes | Cook time: 8 minutes | Serves 6 to 8

- Buttermilk Dressing:
- 60 ml buttermilk
- 60 g chopped spring onions
- 180 ml mayonnaise
- 120 ml sour cream
- ½ teaspoon cayenne pepper
- ½ teaspoon onion powder
- ½ teaspoon garlic powder
- 1 tablespoon chopped chives
- 2 tablespoons chopped fresh dill
- Rock salt and ground black pepper, to taste
- Fried Dill Pickles:
- 90 g plain flour
- 1 (900 g) jar kosher dill pickles, cut into 4 spears, drained
- 300 g panko breadcrumbs
- 2 eggs, beaten with 2 tablespoons water
- Rock salt and ground black pepper, to taste

✧ Cooking spray

Instructions

1. Preheat the air fryer to 200°C 2.Combine the ingredients for the dressing in a bowl 3.Stir to mix well 4.Wrap the bowl in plastic and refrigerate for 30 minutes or until ready to serve 5.Pour the flour in a bowl and sprinkle with salt and ground black pepper 6.Stir to mix well 7.Put the breadcrumbs in a separate bowl 8.Pour the beaten eggs in a third bowl 9.Dredge the pickle spears in the flour, then into the eggs, and then into the panko to coat well 10.Shake the excess off 1Instructions

1.Arrange the pickle spears in a single layer in the preheated air fryer and spritz with cooking spray 12.Air fry for 8 minutes 13.Flip the pickle spears halfway through 14.Serve the pickle spears with buttermilk dressing.

Onion Pakoras

Preparation time: 30 minutes | Cook time: 10 minutes per batch | Serves 2

✧ two medium-sized brown or white onions, sliced (475 g)
✧ 30 g finely chopped fresh coriander
✧ 2 tablespoons mixed vegetables oil
✧ 1 tablespoon gram flour
✧ 1 tablespoon rice flour, or 2 tablespoons gram flour
✧ 1 teaspoon turmeric powder
✧ 1 teaspoon cumin seeds
✧ 1 teaspoon rock salt
✧ ½ teaspoon cayenne pepper
✧ mixed vegetables oil spray

Instructions

1. In a large bowl, combine the onions, coriander, oil, gram flour, rice flour, turmeric, cumin seeds, salt, and cayenne. Stir to combine. Cover and let stand for 30 minutes or up to overnight. (This allows the onions to release moisture, creating a batter.) Mix well before using. 2. Spray the air fryer basket generously with mixed vegetables oil spray.

Drop half of the batter in 6 heaped tablespoons into the basket. Set the air fryer to 180°C for 8 minutes. Carefully turn the pakoras over and spray with oil spray. Set the air fryer for 2 minutes, or until the batter is fully cooked and crisp. 3. Repeat with remaining batter to make 6 more pakoras, checking at 6 minutes for degree of doneness. Serve hot.

Old Bay Chicken Wings

Preparation time: 10 minutes | Cook time: 12 to 15 minutes | Serves 4

✧ 2 tablespoons Old Bay or all-purpose seasoning
✧ 2 teaspoons baking powder
✧ 2 teaspoons salt
✧ 900 g chicken wings, patted dry
✧ Cooking spray

Instructions

1. Preheat the air fryer to 200°C. Lightly spray the air fryer basket with cooking spray. 2. Combine the seasoning, baking powder, and salt in a large zip-top plastic bag. Add the chicken wings, seal, and shake until the wings are thoroughly coated in the seasoning mixture. 3. Lay the chicken wings in the air fryer basket in a single layer and lightly mist with cooking spray. You may need to work in batches to avoid overcrowding. 4. Air fry for 12 to 15 minutes, flipping the wings halfway through, or until the wings are lightly browned and the internal temperature reaches at least 74°C on a meat thermometer. 5. Remove from the basket to a plate and repeat with the remaining chicken wings. 6. Serve hot.

Air Fryer Popcorn with Garlic Salt

Preparation time: 3 minutes | Cook time: 10 minutes | Serves 2

✧ 2 tablespoons olive oil
✧ 60 g popcorn kernels
✧ 1 teaspoon garlic salt

Instructions

1. Preheat the air fryer to 190°C. 2. Tear a square of aluminium foil the size of the bottom of the air fryer and place into the air fryer. 3. Drizzle olive oil over the top of the foil, and then pour in the popcorn kernels. 4. Roast for 8 to 10 minutes, or until the popcorn stops popping. 5. Transfer the popcorn to a large bowl and sprinkle with garlic salt before serving.

Prawns Pirogues

Preparation time: 15 minutes | Cook time: 4 to 5 minutes | Serves 8

- 340 g small, peeled, and deveined raw prawns
- 85 g soft white cheese, at room temperature
- 2 tablespoons natural yoghurt
- 1 teaspoon lemon juice
- 1 teaspoon dried fresh dill, crushed
- Salt, to taste
- 4 small English cucumbers, each approximately 6 inches long

Instructions

1. Pour 4 tablespoons water in bottom of air fryer drawer. 2. Place prawns in air fryer basket in single layer and air fry at 200°C for 4 to 5 minutes, just until done. Watch carefully because prawns cooks quickly, and overcooking makes it tough. 3. Chop prawns into small pieces, no larger than ½ inch. Refrigerate while mixing the remaining ingredients. 4. With a fork, mash and whip the soft white cheese until smooth. 5. Stir in the yoghurt and beat until smooth. Stir in lemon juice, fresh dill, and chopped prawns. 6. Taste for seasoning. If needed, add ¼ to ½ teaspoon salt to suit your taste. 7. Store in refrigerator until serving time. 8. When ready to serve, wash and dry cucumbers and split them lengthwise. Scoop out the seeds and turn cucumbers upside down on kitchen roll to drain for 10 minutes. 9. Just before filling,

wipe centres of cucumbers dry. Spoon the prawns mixture into the pirogues and cut in half crosswise. Serve immediately.

Skinny Fries

Preparation time: 10 minutes | Cook time: 15 minutes per batch | Serves 2

- 2 to 3 russet potatoes or Maris Piper potatoes, peeled and cut into ¼-inch sticks
- 2 to 3 teaspoons olive or mixed vegetables oil
- Salt, to taste

Instructions

1. Cut the potatoes into ¼-inch strips. (A mandolin with a julienne blade is really helpful here.) Rinse the potatoes with cold water several times and let them soak in cold water for at least 10 minutes or as long as overnight. 2. Preheat the air fryer to 190°C. 3. Drain and dry the potato sticks really well, using a clean kitchen towel. Toss the fries with the oil in a bowl and then air fry the fries in two batches at 190°C for 15 minutes, shaking the basket a couple of times while they cook. 4. Add the first batch of crisps back into the air fryer basket with the finishing batch and let everything warm through for a few minutes. As soon as the fries are done, season them with salt and transfer to a plate or basket. Serve them warm with tomato ketchup or your favourite dip.

Lemony Endive in Curried Yoghurt

Preparation time: 5 minutes | Cook time: 10 minutes | Serves 6

- 6 heads endive
- 120 ml plain and fat-free yoghurt
- 3 tablespoons lemon juice
- 1 teaspoon garlic powder
- ½ teaspoon curry powder
- Salt and ground black pepper, to taste

Instructions

1. Wash the endives and slice them in half lengthwise. 2. In a bowl, mix together the yoghurt, lemon juice, garlic powder, curry powder, salt and pepper. 3. Brush the endive halves with the marinade, coating them completely. Allow to sit for at least 30 minutes or up to 24 hours. 4. Preheat the air fryer to 160°C. 5. Put the endives in the air fryer basket and air fry for 10 minutes. 6. Serve hot.

Roasted Grape Dip

Preparation time: 10 minutes | Cook time: 8 to 12 minutes | Serves 6

- ✧ 475 g seedless red grapes, rinsed and patted dry
- ✧ 1 tablespoon apple cider vinegar
- ✧ 1 tablespoon honey
- ✧ 240 ml low-fat Greek yoghurt
- ✧ 2 tablespoons semi-skimmed milk
- ✧ 2 tablespoons minced fresh basil

Instructions

1. In the air fryer basket, sprinkle the grapes with the cider vinegar and drizzle with the honey. Toss to coat. Roast the grapes at 190°C for 8 to 12 minutes, or until shrivelled but still soft. Remove from the air fryer. 2. In a medium-sized bowl, stir together the yoghurt and milk. 3. Gently blend in the grapes and basil. Serve immediately or cover and chill for 1 to 2 hours.

Classic Spring Rolls

Preparation time: 10 minutes | Cook time: 9 minutes | Makes 16 spring rolls

- ✧ 4 teaspoons toasted sesame oil
- ✧ 6 medium garlic cloves, minced or pressed
- ✧ 1 tablespoon grated peeled fresh ginger
- ✧ 70 g thinly sliced shiitake mushrooms
- ✧ 500 g chopped green cabbage
- ✧ 80 g grated carrot
- ✧ ½ teaspoon sea salt

- ✧ 16 rice paper wrappers
- ✧ Cooking oil spray (sunflower, safflower, or refined coconut)
- ✧ Gluten-free sweet and sour sauce or Thai sweet chilli sauce, for serving (optional)

Instructions

1. Place a wok or sauté pan over medium heat until hot. 2. Add the sesame oil, garlic, ginger, mushrooms, cabbage, carrot, and salt. Cook for 3 to 4 minutes, stirring often, until the cabbage is lightly wilted. Remove the pan from the heat. 3. Gently run a rice paper under water. Lay it on a flat non-absorbent surface. Place about 30 g of the cabbage filling in the middle. Once the wrapper is soft enough to roll, fold the bottom up over the filling, fold in the sides, and roll the wrapper all the way up. (Basically, make a tiny burrito.) 4. Repeat step 3 to make the remaining spring rolls until you have the number of spring rolls you want to cook right now (and the amount that will fit in the air fryer basket in a single layer without them touching each other). Refrigerate any leftover filling in an airtight container for about 1 week. 5. Insert the crisper plate into the basket and the basket into the unit. Preheat the unit by selecting AIR FRY, setting the temperature to 200°C, and setting the time to 3 minutes. Select START/STOP to begin. 6. Once the unit is preheated, spray the crisper plate and the basket with cooking oil. Place the spring rolls into the basket, leaving a little room between them so they don't stick to each other. Spray the top of each spring roll with cooking oil. 7. Select AIR FRY, set the temperature to 200°C, and set the time to 9 minutes. Select START/STOP to begin. 8. When the cooking is complete, the egg rolls should be crisp-ish and lightly browned. Serve immediately, plain or with a sauce of choice.

Crispy Mozzarella Cheese Sticks

Preparation time: 8 minutes | Cook time: 5 minutes | Serves 4

- ✧ 65 g plain flour
- ✧ 1 egg, beaten
- ✧ 25 g panko breadcrumbs
- ✧ 30 g grated Parmesan cheese
- ✧ 1 teaspoon Italian seasoning
- ✧ ½ teaspoon garlic salt
- ✧ 6 mozzarella cheese sticks, halved crosswise
- ✧ Olive oil spray

Instructions

1. Put the flour in a small bowl. 2. Put the beaten egg in another small bowl. 3. In a medium-sized bowl, stir together the panko, Parmesan cheese, Italian seasoning, and garlic salt. 4. Roll a mozzarella cheese-stick half in the flour, dip it into the egg, and then roll it in the panko mixture to coat. Press the coating lightly to make sure the breadcrumbs stick to the cheese. Repeat with the remaining 11 mozzarella cheese sticks. 5. Insert the crisper plate into the basket and the basket into the unit. Preheat the unit by selecting AIR FRY, setting the temperature to 200°C, and setting the time to 3 minutes. Select START/STOP to begin. 6. Once the unit is preheated, spray the crisper plate with olive oil and place a baking paper paper liner in the basket. Place the mozzarella cheese sticks into the basket and lightly spray them with olive oil. 7. Select AIR FRY, set the temperature to 200°C, and set the time to 5 minutes. Select START/STOP to begin. 8. When the cooking is complete, the mozzarella cheese sticks should be golden and crispy. Let the sticks stand for 1 minute before transferring them to a serving plate. Serve warm.

Turkey Burger Sliders

Preparation time: 10 minutes | Cook time: 5 to 7 minutes | Makes 8 sliders

- ✧ 450 g finely chopped turkey
- ✧ ¼ teaspoon curry powder
- ✧ 1 teaspoon Hoisin sauce
- ✧ ½ teaspoon salt
- ✧ 8 mini rolls
- ✧ 60 g thinly sliced red onions
- ✧ 60 g slivered green or red pepper
- ✧ 100 g fresh diced pineapple
- ✧ Light soft white cheese

Instructions

1. Combine turkey, curry powder, Hoisin sauce, and salt and mix together well. 2. Shape turkey mixture into 8 small burger patties. 3. Place burger patties in air fryer basket and air fry at 180°C for 5 to 7 minutes, until burger patties are well done, and the juices are clear. 4. Place each patty on the bottom half of a slider roll and top with onions, peppers, and pineapple. Spread the remaining bun halves with soft white cheese to taste, place on top, and serve.

Parmesan-Rosemary Radishes

Preparation time: 5 minutes | Cook time: 15 to 20 minutes | Serves 4

- 1 bunch radishes, stemmed, trimmed, and quartered
- 1 tablespoon avocado oil
- 2 tablespoons finely grated fresh Parmesan cheese
- 1 tablespoon chopped fresh rosemary
- Sea salt and freshly ground black pepper, to taste

Instructions

1. Place the radishes in a medium bowl and toss them with the avocado oil, Parmesan cheese, rosemary, salt, and pepper. 2. Set the air fryer to190ºC. Arrange the radishes in a single layer in the air fryer basket. Roast for 15 to 20 minutes, until golden brown and tender. Let cool for 5 minutes before serving.

Crispy Runner Beans

Preparation time: 5 minutes | Cook time: 8 minutes | Serves 4

- 2 teaspoons olive oil
- 230 g fresh runner beans, ends trimmed
- ¼ teaspoon salt
- ¼ teaspoon ground black pepper

Instructions

1. In a large bowl, drizzle olive oil over runner beans and sprinkle with salt and pepper. 2. Place runner beans into ungreased air fryer basket. Adjust the temperature to 180ºC and set the timer for 8 minutes, shaking the basket two times during cooking. Green beans will be dark golden and crispy at the edges when done. Serve warm.

Sesame Taj Tofu

Preparation time: 5 minutes | Cook time: 25 minutes | Serves 4

- 1 block firm tofu, pressed and cut into 1-inch thick cubes
- 2 tablespoons soy sauce
- 2 teaspoons toasted sesame seeds
- 1 teaspoon rice vinegar
- 1 tablespoon cornflour

Instructions

1. Preheat the air fryer to 200ºC. 2. Add the tofu, soy sauce, sesame seeds, and rice vinegar in a bowl together and mix well to coat the tofu cubes. Then cover the tofu in cornflour and put it in the air fryer basket. 3. Air fry for 25 minutes, giving the basket a shake at five-minute intervals to ensure the tofu cooks evenly. 4. Serve immediately.

Scalloped Potatoes

Preparation time: 5 minutes | Cook time: 20 minutes | Serves 4

- 440 g sliced frozen potatoes, thawed
- 3 cloves garlic, minced
- Pinch salt
- Freshly ground black pepper, to taste
- 180 g double cream

Instructions

1. Preheat the air fryer to 190ºC. 2. Toss the potatoes with the garlic, salt, and black pepper in a baking pan until evenly coated. Pour the double cream over the top. 3. Place the baking pan in the air fryer basket and bake for 15 minutes, or until the potatoes are tender and top is golden brown. Check for doneness and bake for another 5 minutes as needed. 4. Serve hot.

Creamed Asparagus

Preparation time: 10 minutes | Cook time: 18 minutes | Serves 4

- 120 g whipping cream
- 45 g grated Parmesan cheese

- 60 g cream cheese, softened
- 450 g asparagus, ends trimmed, chopped into 1-inch pieces
- ¼ teaspoon salt
- ¼ teaspoon ground black pepper

Instructions

1. In a medium bowl, whisk together whipping cream, Parmesan, and cream cheese until combined. 2. Place asparagus into an ungreased round nonstick baking dish. Pour cheese mixture over top and sprinkle with salt and pepper. 3. Place dish into air fryer basket. Adjust the temperature to 180°C and set the timer for 18 minutes. Asparagus will be tender when done. Serve warm.

Garlic Herb Radishes

Preparation time: 10 minutes | Cook time: 10 minutes | Serves 4

- 450 g radishes
- 2 tablespoons unsalted butter, melted
- ½ teaspoon garlic powder
- ½ teaspoon dried parsley
- ¼ teaspoon dried oregano
- ¼ teaspoon ground black pepper

Instructions

1. Remove roots from radishes and cut into quarters. 2. In a small bowl, add butter and seasonings. Toss the radishes in the herb butter and place into the air fryer basket. 3. Adjust the temperature to 180°C and set the timer for 10 minutes. 4. Halfway through the cooking time, toss the radishes in the air fryer basket. Continue cooking until edges begin to turn brown. 5. Serve warm.

Garlic Courgette and Red Peppers

Preparation time: 5 minutes | Cook time: 15 minutes | Serves 6

- 2 medium courgette, cubed
- 1 red pepper, diced
- 2 garlic cloves, sliced
- 2 tablespoons olive oil

- ½ teaspoon salt

Instructions

1. Preheat the air fryer to 193°C. 2. In a large bowl, mix together the courgette, pepper, and garlic with the olive oil and salt. 3. Pour the mixture into the air fryer basket, and roast for 7 minutes. Shake or stir, then roast for 7 to 8 minutes more.

Spinach and Cheese Stuffed Tomatoes

Preparation time: 20 minutes | Cook time: 15 minutes | Serves 2

- 4 ripe beefsteak tomatoes
- ¾ teaspoon black pepper
- ½ teaspoon coarse sea salt
- 1 (280 g) package frozen chopped spinach, thawed and squeezed dry
- 1 (150 g) package garlic-and-herb Boursin cheese
- 3 tablespoons sour cream
- 45 g finely grated Parmesan cheese

Instructions

1. Cut the tops off the tomatoes. Using a small spoon, carefully remove and discard the pulp. Season the insides with ½ teaspoon of the black pepper and ¼ teaspoon of the salt. Invert the tomatoes onto paper towels and allow to drain while you make the filling. 2. Meanwhile, in a medium bowl, combine the spinach, Boursin cheese, sour cream, ½ of the Parmesan, and the remaining ¼ teaspoon salt and ¼ teaspoon pepper. Stir until ingredients are well combined. Divide the filling among the tomatoes. Top with the remaining ½ of the Parmesan. 3. Place the tomatoes in the air fryer basket. Set the air fryer to 180°C for 15 minutes, or until the filling is hot.

Curry Roasted Cauliflower

Preparation time: 10 minutes | Cook time: 20 minutes | Serves 4

- 65 ml olive oil

- ✧ 2 teaspoons curry powder
- ✧ ½ teaspoon salt
- ✧ ¼ teaspoon freshly ground black pepper
- ✧ 1 head cauliflower, cut into bite-size florets
- ✧ ½ red onion, sliced
- ✧ 2 tablespoons freshly chopped parsley, for garnish (optional)

Instructions

1. Preheat the air fryer to 200°C. 2. In a large bowl, combine the olive oil, curry powder, salt, and pepper. Add the cauliflower and onion. Toss gently until the vegetables are completely coated with the oil mixture. Transfer the vegetables to the basket of the air fryer. 3. Pausing about halfway through the cooking time to shake the basket, air fry for 20 minutes until the cauliflower is tender and beginning to brown. Top with the parsley, if desired, before serving.

Citrus Sweet Potatoes and Carrots

Preparation time: 5 minutes | Cook time: 20 to 25 minutes | Serves 4

- ✧ 2 large carrots, cut into 1-inch chunks
- ✧ 1 medium sweet potato, peeled and cut into 1-inch cubes
- ✧ 25 g chopped onion
- ✧ 2 garlic cloves, minced
- ✧ 2 tablespoons honey
- ✧ 1 tablespoon freshly squeezed orange juice
- ✧ 2 teaspoons butter, melted

Instructions

1. Insert the crisper plate into the basket and the basket into the unit. Preheat the unit by selecting AIR ROAST, setting the temperature to 200°C, and setting the time to 3 minutes. Select START/STOP to begin. 2. In a 6-by-2-inch round pan, toss together the carrots, sweet potato, onion, garlic, honey, orange juice, and melted butter to coat. 3. Once the unit is preheated, place the pan into the basket. 4. Select AIR ROAST, set the

temperature to 200°C, and set the time to 25 minutes. Select START/STOP to begin. 5. After 15 minutes, remove the basket and shake the vegetables. Reinsert the basket to resume cooking. After 5 minutes, if the vegetables are tender and glazed, they are done. If not, resume cooking. 6. When the cooking is complete, serve immediately.

Hasselback Potatoes with Chive Pesto

Preparation time: 10 minutes | Cook time: 40 minutes | Serves 2

- ✧ 2 medium Maris Piper potatoes
- ✧ 5 tablespoons olive oil
- ✧ coarse sea salt and freshly ground black pepper, to taste
- ✧ 10 g roughly chopped fresh chives
- ✧ 2 tablespoons packed fresh flat-leaf parsley leaves
- ✧ 1 tablespoon chopped walnuts
- ✧ 1 tablespoon grated Parmesan cheese
- ✧ 1 teaspoon fresh lemon juice
- ✧ 1 small garlic clove, peeled
- ✧ 60 g sour cream

Instructions

1. Place the potatoes on a cutting board and lay a chopstick or thin-handled wooden spoon to the side of each potato. Thinly slice the potatoes crosswise, letting the chopstick or spoon handle stop the blade of your knife, and stop ½ inch short of each end of the potato. Rub the potatoes with 1 tablespoon of the olive oil and season with salt and pepper. 2. Place the potatoes, cut-side up, in the air fryer and air fry at 190°C until golden brown and crisp on the outside and tender inside, about 40 minutes, drizzling the insides with 1 tablespoon more olive oil and seasoning with more salt and pepper halfway through. 3. Meanwhile, in a small blender or food processor, combine the remaining 3 tablespoons olive oil, the chives, parsley,

walnuts, Parmesan, lemon juice, and garlic and purée until smooth. Season the chive pesto with salt and pepper. 4. Remove the potatoes from the air fryer and transfer to plates. Drizzle the potatoes with the pesto, letting it drip down into the grooves, then dollop each with sour cream and serve hot.

Sweet and Crispy Roasted Pearl Onions

Preparation time: 5 minutes | Cook time: 18 minutes | Serves 3

- ✧ 1 (410 g) package frozen pearl onions (do not thaw)
- ✧ 2 tablespoons extra-virgin olive oil
- ✧ 2 tablespoons balsamic vinegar
- ✧ 2 teaspoons finely chopped fresh rosemary
- ✧ ½ teaspoon coarse sea salt
- ✧ ¼ teaspoon black pepper

Instructions

1. In a medium bowl, combine the onions, olive oil, vinegar, rosemary, salt, and pepper until well coated. 2. Transfer the onions to the air fryer basket. Set the air fryer to 200ºC for 18 minutes, or until the onions are tender and lightly charred, stirring once or twice during the cooking time.

Cauliflower with Lime Juice

Preparation time: 10 minutes | Cook time: 7 minutes | Serves 4

- ✧ 215 g chopped cauliflower florets
- ✧ 2 tablespoons coconut oil, melted
- ✧ 2 teaspoons chilli powder
- ✧ ½ teaspoon garlic powder
- ✧ 1 medium lime
- ✧ 2 tablespoons chopped coriander

Instructions

1. In a large bowl, toss cauliflower with coconut oil. Sprinkle with chilli powder and garlic powder. Place seasoned cauliflower into the air fryer basket. 2. Adjust the temperature to 180ºC and set the timer for 7

minutes. 3. Cauliflower will be tender and begin to turn golden at the edges. Place into a serving bowl. 4. Cut the lime into quarters and squeeze juice over cauliflower. Garnish with coriander.

Cauliflower Rice Balls

Preparation time: 10 minutes | Cook time: 8 minutes | Serves 4

- ✧ 1 (280 g) steamer bag cauliflower rice, cooked according to package instructions
- ✧ 110 g shredded Mozzarella cheese
- ✧ 1 large egg
- ✧ 60 g plain pork scratchings, finely crushed
- ✧ ¼ teaspoon salt
- ✧ ½ teaspoon Italian seasoning

Instructions

1. Place cauliflower into a large bowl and mix with Mozzarella. 2. Whisk egg in a separate medium bowl. Place pork scratchings into another large bowl with salt and Italian seasoning. 3. Separate cauliflower mixture into four equal sections and form each into a ball. Carefully dip a ball into whisked egg, then roll in pork scratchings. Repeat with remaining balls. 4. Place cauliflower balls into ungreased air fryer basket. Adjust the temperature to 200ºC and air fry for 8 minutes. Rice balls will be golden when done. 5. Use a spatula to carefully move cauliflower balls to a large dish for serving. Serve warm.

Mole-Braised Cauliflower

Preparation time: 10 minutes | Cook time: 15 minutes | Serves 2

- ✧ 230 g medium cauliflower florets
- ✧ 1 tablespoon vegetable oil
- ✧ coarse sea salt and freshly ground black pepper, to taste
- ✧ 350 ml vegetable stock
- ✧ 2 tablespoons New Mexico chilli powder (or regular chilli powder)

- ❖ 2 tablespoons salted roasted peanuts
- ❖ 1 tablespoon toasted sesame seeds, plus more for garnish
- ❖ 1 tablespoon finely chopped golden raisins
- ❖ 1 teaspoon coarse sea salt
- ❖ 1 teaspoon dark brown sugar
- ❖ ½ teaspoon dried oregano
- ❖ ¼ teaspoon cayenne pepper
- ❖ ⅛ teaspoon ground cinnamon

Instructions

1. In a large bowl, toss the cauliflower with the oil and season with salt and black pepper. Transfer to a cake pan. Place the pan in the air fryer and roast at 190ºC until the cauliflower is tender and lightly browned at the edges, about 10 minutes, stirring halfway through. 2. Meanwhile, in a small blender, combine the stock, chilli powder, peanuts, sesame seeds, raisins, salt, brown sugar, oregano, cayenne, and cinnamon and purée until smooth. Pour into a small saucepan or frying pan and bring to a simmer over medium heat, then cook until reduced by half, 3 to 5 minutes. 3. Pour the hot mole sauce over the cauliflower in the pan, stir to coat, then cook until the sauce is thickened and lightly charred on the cauliflower, about 5 minutes more. Sprinkle with more sesame seeds and serve warm.

Spiced Honey-Walnut Carrots

Preparation time: 5 minutes | Cook time: 12 minutes | Serves 6

- ❖ 450 g baby carrots
- ❖ 2 tablespoons olive oil
- ❖ 80 g raw honey
- ❖ ¼ teaspoon ground cinnamon
- ❖ 25 g black walnuts, chopped

Instructions

1. Preheat the air fryer to 180ºC. 2. In a large bowl, toss the baby carrots with olive oil, honey, and cinnamon until well coated. 3. Pour into the air fryer and roast for 6

minutes. Shake the basket, sprinkle the walnuts on top, and roast for 6 minutes more. 4. Remove the carrots from the air fryer and serve.

Asparagus Fries

Preparation time: 15 minutes | Cook time: 5 to 7 minutes per batch | Serves 4

- ❖ 340 g fresh asparagus spears with tough ends trimmed off
- ❖ 2 egg whites
- ❖ 60 ml water
- ❖ 80 g panko bread crumbs
- ❖ 25 g grated Parmesan cheese, plus 2 tablespoons
- ❖ ¼ teaspoon salt
- ❖ Oil for misting or cooking spray

Instructions

1. Preheat the air fryer to 200ºC. 2. In a shallow dish, beat egg whites and water until slightly foamy. 3. In another shallow dish, combine panko, Parmesan, and salt. 4. Dip asparagus spears in egg, then roll in crumbs. Spray with oil or cooking spray. 5. Place a layer of asparagus in air fryer basket, leaving just a little space in between each spear. Stack another layer on top, crosswise. Air fry at 200ºC for 5 to 7 minutes, until crispy and golden brown. 6. Repeat to cook remaining asparagus.

Fried Asparagus

Preparation time: 5 minutes | Cook time: 12 minutes | Serves 4

- ❖ 1 tablespoon olive oil
- ❖ 450 g asparagus spears, ends trimmed
- ❖ ¼ teaspoon salt
- ❖ ¼ teaspoon ground black pepper
- ❖ 1 tablespoon salted butter, melted

Instructions

1. In a large bowl, drizzle olive oil over asparagus spears and sprinkle with salt and pepper. 2. Place spears into ungreased air

fryer basket. Adjust the temperature to 190ºC and set the timer for 12 minutes, shaking the basket halfway through cooking. Asparagus will be lightly browned and tender when done. 3. Transfer to a large dish and drizzle with butter. Serve warm.

Easy Rosemary Runner Beans

Preparation time: 5 minutes | Cook time: 5 minutes | Serves 1

- ✧ 1 tablespoon butter, melted
- ✧ 2 tablespoons rosemary
- ✧ ½ teaspoon salt
- ✧ 3 cloves garlic, minced
- ✧ 95 g chopped runner beans

Instructions

1. Preheat the air fryer to 200ºC. 2. Combine the melted butter with the rosemary, salt, and minced garlic. Toss in the runner beans, coating them well. 3. Air fry for 5 minutes. 4. Serve immediately.

Mashed Sweet Potato Tots

Preparation time: 10 minutes | Cook time: 12 to 13 minutes per batch | Makes 18 to 24 tots

- ✧ 210 g cooked mashed sweet potatoes
- ✧ 1 egg white, beaten
- ✧ ⅛ teaspoon ground cinnamon
- ✧ 1 dash nutmeg
- ✧ 2 tablespoons chopped pecans
- ✧ 1½ teaspoons honey
- ✧ Salt, to taste
- ✧ 50 g panko bread crumbs
- ✧ Oil for misting or cooking spray

Instructions

1. Preheat the air fryer to 200ºC. 2. In a large bowl, mix together the potatoes, egg white, cinnamon, nutmeg, pecans, honey, and salt to taste. 3. Place panko crumbs on a sheet of wax paper. 4. For each tot, use about 2 teaspoons of sweet potato mixture. To shape, drop the measure of potato mixture onto panko crumbs and push crumbs up and around potatoes to coat edges. Then turn tot over to coat other side with crumbs. 5. Mist tots with oil or cooking spray and place in air fryer basket in single layer. 6. Air fry at 200ºC for 12 to 13 minutes, until browned and crispy. 7. Repeat steps 5 and 6 to cook remaining tots.

Roasted Brussels Sprouts with Bacon

Preparation time: 10 minutes | Cook time: 20 minutes | Serves 4

- ✧ 4 slices thick-cut bacon, chopped (about 110 g)
- ✧ 450 g Brussels sprouts, halved (or quartered if large)
- ✧ Freshly ground black pepper, to taste

Instructions

1. Preheat the air fryer to 190ºC. 2. Air fry the bacon for 5 minutes, shaking the basket once or twice during the cooking time. 3. Add the Brussels sprouts to the basket and drizzle a little bacon fat from the bottom of the air fryer drawer into the basket. Toss the sprouts to coat with the bacon fat. Air fry for an additional 15 minutes, or until the Brussels sprouts are tender to a knifepoint. 4. Season with freshly ground black pepper.

Buffalo Cauliflower with Blue Cheese

Preparation time: 15 minutes | Cook time: 5 to 7 minutes per batch | Serves 6

- ✧ 1 large head cauliflower, rinsed and separated into small florets
- ✧ 1 tablespoon extra-virgin olive oil
- ✧ ½ teaspoon garlic powder
- ✧ Cooking oil spray
- ✧ 80 ml hot wing sauce
- ✧ 190 g nonfat Greek yoghurt
- ✧ 60 g buttermilk
- ✧ ½ teaspoon hot sauce
- ✧ 1 celery stick, chopped

✧ 2 tablespoons crumbled blue cheese

Instructions

1. Insert the crisper plate into the basket and the basket into the unit. Preheat the unit by selecting AIR FRY, setting the temperature to190°C, and setting the time to 3 minutes. Select START/STOP to begin. 2. In a large bowl, toss together the cauliflower florets and olive oil. Sprinkle with the garlic powder and toss again to coat. 3. Once the unit is preheated, spray the crisper plate with cooking oil. Put half the cauliflower into the basket. 4. Select AIR FRY, set the temperature to190°C, and set the time to 7 minutes. Select START/STOP to begin. 5. After 3 minutes, remove the basket and shake the cauliflower. Reinsert the basket to resume cooking. After 2 minutes, check the cauliflower. It is done when it is browned. If not, resume cooking. 6. When the cooking is complete, transfer the cauliflower to a serving bowl and toss with half the hot wing sauce. 7. Repeat steps 4, 5, and 6 with the remaining cauliflower and hot wing sauce. 8. In a small bowl, stir together the yoghurt, buttermilk, hot sauce, celery, and blue cheese. Drizzle the sauce over the finished cauliflower and serve.

Super Vegetable Burger

Preparation time: 15 minutes | Cook time: 12 minutes | Serves 8

- ✧ 230 g cauliflower, steamed and diced, rinsed and drained
- ✧ 2 teaspoons coconut oil, melted
- ✧ 2 teaspoons minced garlic
- ✧ 60 g desiccated coconut
- ✧ 120 g oats
- ✧ 3 tablespoons flour
- ✧ 1 tablespoon flaxseeds plus 3 tablespoons water, divided
- ✧ 1 teaspoon mustard powder
- ✧ 2 teaspoons thyme
- ✧ 2 teaspoons parsley
- ✧ 2 teaspoons chives
- ✧ Salt and ground black pepper, to taste
- ✧ 235 g breadcrumbs

Instructions

1. Preheat the air fryer to 200°C. 2.Combine the cauliflower with all the ingredients, except for the breadcrumbs, incorporating everything well. 3.Using the hands, shape 8 equal-sized amounts of the mixture into burger patties. 4.Coat the patties in breadcrumbs before putting them in the air fryer basket in a single layer. 5.Air fry for 12 minutes or until crispy. 6.Serve hot.

Basmati Risotto

Preparation time: 10 minutes | Cook time: 30 minutes | Serves 2

- ✧ 1 onion, diced
- ✧ 1 small carrot, diced
- ✧ 475 ml vegetable broth, boiling
- ✧ 120 g grated Cheddar cheese
- ✧ 1 clove garlic, minced
- ✧ 180 g long-grain basmati rice
- ✧ 1 tablespoon olive oil

- ✧ 1 tablespoon unsalted butter

Instructions

1. Preheat the air fryer to 200°C. 2.Grease a baking tin with oil and stir in the butter, garlic, carrot, and onion. 3.Put the tin in the air fryer and bake for 4 minutes. 4.Pour in the rice and bake for a further 4 minutes, stirring three times throughout the baking time. 5.Turn the temperature down to 160°C. 6.Add the vegetable broth and give the dish a gentle stir. 7.Bake for 22 minutes, leaving the air fryer uncovered. 8.Pour in the cheese, stir once more and serve.

Sweet Potatoes with Courgette

Preparation time: 20 minutes | Cook time: 20 minutes | Serves 4

- ✧ 2 large-sized sweet potatoes, peeled and quartered
- ✧ 1 medium courgette, sliced
- ✧ 1 Serrano or red chilli, deseeded and thinly sliced
- ✧ 1 pepper, deseeded and thinly sliced
- ✧ 1 to 2 carrots, cut into matchsticks
- ✧ 60 ml olive oil
- ✧ 1½ tablespoons maple syrup
- ✧ ½ teaspoon porcini powder or paste
- ✧ ¼ teaspoon mustard powder
- ✧ ½ teaspoon fennel seeds
- ✧ 1 tablespoon garlic powder
- ✧ ½ teaspoon fine sea salt
- ✧ ¼ teaspoon ground black pepper
- ✧ Tomato ketchup, for serving

Instructions

1. Put the sweet potatoes, courgette, peppers, and the carrot into the air fryer basket. 2.Coat with a drizzling of olive oil. 3.Preheat the air fryer to 180°C. 4.Air fry the vegetables for 15 minutes. 5.In the meantime, prepare the sauce by vigorously combining the other

ingredients, except for the tomato ketchup, with a whisk. 6.Lightly grease a baking dish. 7.Transfer the cooked vegetables to the baking dish, pour over the sauce and coat the vegetables well. 8.Increase the temperature to 200ºC and air fry the vegetables for an additional 5 minutes. 9.Serve warm with a side of ketchup.

Parmesan Artichokes

Preparation time: 10 minutes | Cook time: 10 minutes | Serves 4

- ✧ 2 medium artichokes, trimmed and quartered, centre removed
- ✧ 2 tablespoons coconut oil
- ✧ 1 large egg, beaten
- ✧ 120 g grated vegetarian Parmesan cheese
- ✧ 60 g blanched finely ground almond flour
- ✧ ½ teaspoon crushed red pepper flakes

Instructions

1. In a large bowl, toss artichokes in coconut oil and then dip each piece into the egg. 2.Mix the Parmesan and almond flour in a large bowl. 3.Add artichoke pieces and toss to cover as completely as possible, sprinkle with pepper flakes. 4.Place into the air fryer basket. 5.Adjust the temperature to 200ºC and air fry for 10 minutes. 6.Toss the basket two times during cooking. 7.Serve warm.

Baked Courgette

Preparation time: 10 minutes | Cook time: 8 minutes | Serves 4

- ✧ 2 tablespoons salted butter
- ✧ 60 g diced white onion
- ✧ ½ teaspoon minced garlic
- ✧ 120 ml double cream
- ✧ 60 g full fat soft white cheese
- ✧ 235 g shredded extra mature Cheddar cheese
- ✧ 2 medium courgette, spiralized

Instructions

1. In a large saucepan over medium heat, melt butter. 2.Add onion and sauté until it begins to soften, 1 to 3 minutes. 3.Add garlic and sauté for 30 seconds, then pour in cream and add soft white cheese. 4.Remove the pan from heat and stir in Cheddar. 5.Add the courgette and toss in the sauce, then put into a round baking dish. 6.Cover the dish with foil and place into the air fryer basket. 7.Adjust the temperature to 190ºC and set the timer for 8 minutes. 8.After 6 minutes remove the foil and let the top brown for remaining cooking time. 9.Stir and serve.

Cauliflower Rice-Stuffed Peppers

Preparation time: 10 minutes | Cook time: 15 minutes | Serves 4

- ✧ 475 g uncooked cauliflower rice
- ✧ 180 g drained canned petite diced tomatoes
- ✧ 2 tablespoons olive oil
- ✧ 235 g shredded Mozzarella cheese
- ✧ ¼ teaspoon salt
- ✧ ¼ teaspoon ground black pepper
- ✧ 4 medium green peppers, tops removed, seeded

Instructions

1. In a large bowl, mix all ingredients except peppers. 2.Scoop mixture evenly into peppers. 3.Place peppers into ungreased air fryer basket. 4.Adjust the temperature to 180ºC and air fry for 15 minutes. 5.Peppers will be tender, and cheese will be melted when done. 6.Serve warm.

Gold Ravioli

Preparation time: 10 minutes | Cook time: 6 minutes | Serves 4

- ✧ 120 g panko breadcrumbs
- ✧ 2 teaspoons Engevita yeast flakes
- ✧ 1 teaspoon dried basil
- ✧ 1 teaspoon dried oregano
- ✧ 1 teaspoon garlic powder
- ✧ Salt and ground black pepper, to taste
- ✧ 60 g aquafaba or egg alternative

- 227 g ravioli
- Cooking spray

Instructions

1. Cover the air fryer basket with aluminium foil and coat with a light brushing of oil. 2.Preheat the air fryer to 200°C. 3.Combine the panko breadcrumbs, Engevita yeast flakes, basil, oregano, and garlic powder. 4.Sprinkle with salt and pepper to taste. 5.Put the aquafaba in a separate bowl. 6.Dip the ravioli in the aquafaba before coating it in the panko mixture. 7.Spritz with cooking spray and transfer to the air fryer. 8.Air fry for 6 minutes. 9.Shake the air fryer basket halfway. 10.Serve hot.

Air Fryer Veggies with Halloumi

Preparation time: 5 minutes | Cook time: 14 minutes | Serves 2

- 2 courgettes, cut into even chunks
- 1 large aubergine, peeled, cut into chunks
- 1 large carrot, cut into chunks
- 170 g halloumi cheese, cubed
- 2 teaspoons olive oil
- Salt and black pepper, to taste
- 1 teaspoon dried mixed herbs

Instructions

1. Preheat the air fryer to 170°C. 2.Combine the courgettes, aubergine, carrot, cheese, olive oil, salt, and pepper in a large bowl and toss to coat well. 3.Spread the mixture evenly in the air fryer basket and air fry for 14 minutes until crispy and golden, shaking the basket once during cooking. 4.Serve topped with mixed herbs.

Mediterranean Creamed Green Peas

Preparation time: 5 minutes | Cook time: 25 minutes | Serves 4

- 235 ml cauliflower florets, fresh or frozen
- ½ white onion, roughly chopped
- 2 tablespoons olive oil
- 120 ml unsweetened almond milk
- 700 ml green peas, fresh or frozen
- 3 garlic cloves, minced
- 2 tablespoons fresh thyme leaves, chopped
- 1 teaspoon fresh rosemary leaves, chopped
- ½ teaspoon salt
- ½ teaspoon black pepper
- Shredded Parmesan cheese, for garnish
- Fresh parsley, for garnish

Instructions

1. Preheat the air fryer to 192°C. 2. In a large bowl, combine the cauliflower florets and onion with the olive oil and toss well to coat. 3. Put the cauliflower-and-onion mixture into the air fryer basket in an even layer and bake for 15 minutes. 4. Transfer the cauliflower and onion to a food processor. 5. Add the almond milk and pulse until smooth. 6. In a medium saucepan, combine the cauliflower purée, peas, garlic, thyme, rosemary, salt, and pepper and mix well. 7. Cook over medium heat for an additional 10 minutes, stirring regularly. 8. Serve with a sprinkle of Parmesan cheese and chopped fresh parsley.

Gluten-Free Spice Cookies

Preparation time: 10 minutes | Cook time: 12 minutes | Serves 4

- ✧ 4 tablespoons unsalted butter, at room temperature
- ✧ 2 tablespoons agave nectar
- ✧ 1 large egg
- ✧ 2 tablespoons water
- ✧ 120 g almond flour
- ✧ 80 g granulated sugar
- ✧ 2 teaspoons ground ginger
- ✧ 1 teaspoon ground cinnamon
- ✧ ½ teaspoon freshly grated nutmeg
- ✧ 1 teaspoon baking soda
- ✧ ¼ teaspoon kosher, or coarse sea salt

Instructions

1. Line the bottom of the air fryer basket with baking paper cut to fit. 2. In a large bowl, using a hand mixer, beat together the butter, agave, egg, and water on medium speed until light and fluffy. 3. Add the almond flour, sugar, ginger, cinnamon, nutmeg, baking soda, and salt. Beat on low speed until well combined. 4. Roll the dough into 2-tablespoon balls and arrange them on the baking paper in the basket. (They don't really spread too much but try to leave a little room between them.) Set the air fryer to 160°C, and cook for 12 minutes, or until the tops of cookies are lightly browned. 5. Transfer to a wire rack and let cool completely. Store in an airtight container for up to a week.

Kentucky Chocolate Nut Pie

Preparation time: 20 minutes | Cook time: 25 minutes | Serves 8

- ✧ 2 large eggs, beaten
- ✧ 75 g unsalted butter, melted
- ✧ 160 g granulated sugar
- ✧ 30 g Plain flour
- ✧ 190 g coarsely chopped pecans
- ✧ 170 g milk chocolate crisps
- ✧ 2 tablespoons bourbon, or peach juice
- ✧ 1 (9-inch) unbaked piecrust

Instructions

1. In a large bowl, stir together the eggs and melted butter. Add the sugar and flour and stir until combined. Stir in the pecans, chocolate crisps, and bourbon until well mixed. 2. Using a fork, prick holes in the bottom and sides of the pie crust. Pour the pie filling into the crust. 3. Preheat the air fryer to 180°C. 4. Cook for 25 minutes, or until a knife inserted into the middle of the pie comes out clean. Let set for 5 minutes before serving.

Luscious Coconut Pie

Preparation time: 5 minutes | Cook time: 45 minutes | Serves 6

- ✧ 100 g desiccated, unsweetened coconut, plus 25 g, divided
- ✧ 2 eggs
- ✧ 355 ml almond milk
- ✧ 100 g granulated sweetener
- ✧ 30 g coconut flour
- ✧ 55 g unsalted butter, melted
- ✧ 1½ teaspoons vanilla extract
- ✧ ¼ teaspoon salt
- ✧ 2 tablespoons powdered sweetener (optional)
- ✧ 120 g whipping cream, whipped until stiff (optional)

Instructions

1. Spread 25 g of the coconut in the bottom of a pie plate and place in the air fryer basket. Set the air fryer to 180°C and air fry the coconut while the air fryer preheats, about 5 minutes, until golden brown. Transfer the

coconut to a small bowl and set aside for garnish. Brush the pie plate with oil and set aside. 2. In a large bowl, combine the remaining 100 g desiccated coconut, eggs, milk, granulated sweetener, coconut flour, butter, vanilla, and salt. Whisk until smooth. Pour the batter into the prepared pie plate and air fry for 40 to 45 minutes, or until a toothpick inserted into the center of the pie comes out clean. (Check halfway through the baking time and rotate the pan, if necessary, for even baking.) 3. Remove the pie from the air fryer and place on a baking rack to cool completely. Garnish with the reserved toasted coconut and the powdered sweetener or whipped cream, if desired. Cover and refrigerate leftover pie for up to 3 days.

Bourbon Bread Pudding

Preparation time: 10 minutes | Cook time: 20 minutes | Serves 4

- ✧ 3 slices whole grain bread, cubed
- ✧ 1 large egg
- ✧ 240 ml whole milk
- ✧ 2 tablespoons bourbon, or peach juice
- ✧ ½ teaspoons vanilla extract
- ✧ 4 tablespoons maple syrup, divided
- ✧ ½ teaspoons ground cinnamon
- ✧ 2 teaspoons sparkling sugar

Instructions

1. Preheat the air fryer to 130°C. 2. Spray a baking pan with nonstick cooking spray, then place the bread cubes in the pan. 3. In a medium bowl, whisk together the egg, milk, bourbon, vanilla extract, 3 tablespoons of maple syrup, and cinnamon. Pour the egg mixture over the bread and press down with a spatula to coat all the bread, then sprinkle the sparkling sugar on top and bake for 20 minutes. 4. Remove the pudding from the air fryer and allow to cool in the pan on a wire rack for 10 minutes. Drizzle the remaining 1 tablespoon of maple syrup on top. Slice and serve warm.

Baked Apple

Preparation time: 10 minutes | Cook time: 20 minutes | Makes 6 apple halves

- ✧ 3 small Pink Lady or other baking apples
- ✧ 3 tablespoons maple syrup
- ✧ 3 tablespoons chopped pecans
- ✧ 1 tablespoon firm butter, cut into 6 pieces

Instructions

1. Put 6½ tablespoons water in the drawer of the air fryer. 2. Wash apples well and dry them. 3. Split apples in half. Remove core and a little of the flesh to make a cavity for the pecans. 4. Place apple halves in air fryer basket, cut side up. 5. Spoon 1½ teaspoons pecans into each cavity. 6. Spoon ½ tablespoon maple syrup over pecans in each apple. 7. Top each apple with 1 piece of butter. 8. Bake at 180°C for 20 minutes, until apples are tender.

Peanut Butter, Honey & Banana Toast

Preparation time: 10 minutes | Cook time: 9 minutes | Serves 4

- ✧ 2 tablespoons unsalted butter, softened
- ✧ 4 slices white bread
- ✧ 4 tablespoons peanut butter
- ✧ 2 bananas, peeled and thinly sliced
- ✧ 4 tablespoons honey
- ✧ 1 teaspoon ground cinnamon

Instructions

1. Spread butter on one side of each slice of bread, then peanut butter on the other side. Arrange the banana slices on top of the peanut butter sides of each slice (about 9 slices per toast). Drizzle honey on top of the banana and sprinkle with cinnamon. 2. Cut each slice in half lengthwise so that it will better fit into the air fryer basket. Arrange two pieces of bread, butter sides down, in the air fryer basket. Set the air fryer to 190°C

cooking for 5 minutes. Then set the air fryer to 200°C and cook for an additional 4 minutes, or until the bananas have started to brown. Repeat with remaining slices. Serve hot.

Coconut Macaroons

Preparation time: 5 minutes | Cook time: 8 to 10 minutes | Makes 12 macaroons

✧ 120 g desiccated coconut
✧ 4½ teaspoons Plain flour
✧ 2 tablespoons sugar
✧ 1 egg white
✧ ½ teaspoon almond extract

Instructions

1. Preheat the air fryer to 160°C. 2. In a medium bowl, mix all ingredients together. 3. Shape coconut mixture into 12 balls. 4. Place all 12 macaroons in air fryer basket. They won't expand, so you tin place them close together, but they shouldn't touch. 5. Air fry for 8 to 10 minutes, until golden.

Cardamom Custard

Preparation time: 10 minutes | Cook time: 25 minutes | Serves 2

✧ 240 ml whole milk
✧ 1 large egg
✧ 2 tablespoons granulated sugar, plus 1 teaspoon
✧ ¼ teaspoon vanilla bean paste or pure vanilla extract
✧ ¼ teaspoon ground cardamom, plus more for sprinkling

Instructions

1. In a medium bowl, beat together the milk, egg, sugar, vanilla, and cardamom. 2. Place two ramekins in the air fryer basket. Divide the mixture between the ramekins. Sprinkle lightly with cardamom. Cover each ramekin tightly with aluminium foil. Set the air fryer to 180°C and cook for 25 minutes, or until a toothpick inserted in the center comes out clean. 3. Let the custards cool on a wire rack for 5 to 10 minutes. 4. Serve warm or refrigerate until cold and serve chilled.

Cherry Pie

Preparation time: 15 minutes | Cook time: 35 minutes | Serves 6

✧ All-purpose flour, for dusting
✧ 1 package of shortcrust pastry, cut in half, at room temperature
✧ 350 g tin cherry pie filling
✧ 1 egg
✧ 1 tablespoon water
✧ 1 tablespoon sugar

Instructions

1. Dust a work surface with flour and place the piecrust on it. Roll out the piecrust. Invert a shallow air fryer baking pan, or your own pie dish that fits inside the air fryer basket, on top of the dough. Trim the dough around the pan, making your cut ½ inch wider than the pan itself. 2. Repeat with the second piecrust but make the cut the same size as or slightly smaller than the pan. 3. Put the larger crust in the bottom of the baking pan. Don't stretch the dough. Gently press it into the pan. 4. Spoon in enough cherry pie filling to fill the crust. Do not overfill. 5. Using a knife or pizza cutter, cut the second piecrust into 1-inch-wide strips. Weave the strips in a lattice pattern over the top of the cherry pie filling. 6. Insert the crisper plate into the basket and the basket into the unit. Preheat to 160°C. 7. In a small bowl, whisk the egg and water. Gently brush the egg wash over the top of the pie. Sprinkle with the sugar and cover the pie with aluminium foil. 8. Once the unit is preheated, place the pie into the basket. 9. Bake for 30 minutes, remove the foil and resume cooking for 3 to 5 minutes more. The finished pie should have a flaky golden-brown crust and bubbling pie filling. 10. When the cooking is complete, serve warm. Refrigerate leftovers for a few

days.

Cream-Filled Sponge Cakes

Preparation time: 10 minutes | Cook time: 10 minutes | Makes 4 cakes

- ✧ Coconut, or avocado oil, for spraying
- ✧ 1 tube croissant dough
- ✧ 4 Swiss rolls
- ✧ 1 tablespoon icing sugar

Instructions

1. Line the air fryer basket with baking paper, and spray lightly with oil. 2. Unroll the dough into a single flat layer and cut it into 4 equal pieces. 3. Place 1 sponge cake in the center of each piece of dough. Wrap the dough around the cake, pinching the ends to seal. 4. Place the wrapped cakes in the prepared basket, and spray lightly with oil. 5. Bake at 90°C for 5 minutes, flip, spray with oil, and cook for another 5 minutes, or until golden brown. 6. Dust with the icing sugar and serve.

APPENDIX 1: MEASUREMENT CONVERSION CHART

Volume Equivalents (Dry):	Temperature Equivalents:
1/8 teaspoon = 0.5 mL	225°F = 107°C
1/4 teaspoon = 1 mL	250°F = 121°C
1/2 teaspoon = 2 mL	275°F = 135°C
3/4 teaspoon = 4 mL	300°F = 149°C
1 teaspoon = 5 mL	325°F = 163°C
1 tablespoon = 15 mL	350°F = 177°C
1/4 cup = 59 mL	375°F = 191°C
1/2 cup = 118 mL	400°F = 204°C
3/4 cup = 177 mL	425°F = 218°C
1 cup = 235 mL	450°F = 232°C
2 cups (or 1 pint) = 475 mL	475°F = 246°C
4 cups (or 1 quart) = 1 L	500°F = 260°C

Weight Equivalents:	Volume Equivalents (Liquid):
1 ounce = 28 g	1/4 cup = 60 mL = 2 fl oz
2 ounces = 57 g	1/2 cup = 120 mL = 4 fl oz
5 ounces = 142 g	1 cup = 240 mL = 8 fl oz
10 ounces = 284 g	2 cups (or 1 pint) = 475 mL = 16 fl oz
15 ounces = 425 g	4 cups (or 1 quart) = 1 L = 32 fl oz
16 ounces (1 pound) = 455 g	1 gallon = 4 L = 128 fl oz
1.5 pounds = 680 g	
2 pounds = 907 g	

Printed in Great Britain
by Amazon

58726490R00044